With my compliments to the Sandy & Jim Bruner

A PORTRIT HISTORY OF THE ROMAN EMPERORS

by William F. Hornyak

Copyright © 1998
William F. Hornyak

All rights reserved. No part of this book may be reproduced
in any form, except for the inclusion of brief quotations in a review,
without permission in writing from the author or publisher.

ISBN: 1-57502-823-9
Library of Congress Catalog Card Number: 98-71758

Printed in the USA by

Morris Publishing

3212 East Highway 30 • Kearney, NE 68847 • 1-800-650-7888

DEDICATION

*To my grandson, Samuel Hornyak Hale.
May he learn to love the Classical Antique world as much
as his grandfather does.*

A PORTRAIT HISTORY
of the
ROMAN EMPERORS
based on
COINS AND MEDALLIONS
(Covering the imperatorial period from 60 B.C. to A.D. 425)

Sooner or later, the serious study of Roman history leads to the desire to obtain at least a few coins struck during the various historical periods. The vast abundance of these issues allows for the ready access to such specimens. These small intriguing works of art and bits of historical evidence may be appreciated at many levels of interest.

In addition to being genuine works of art, coins also inspire an intimate linkage to the peoples of this remarkable civilization that has so profoundly and pervasively influenced the development of Western culture. Viewing the portraits, often shown on coins and medallions, engenders a feeling of close personal contact with the many depicted titans of history.

The inscriptions appearing on both sides of the coins and the motives, particularly those appearing on the reverse sides, offer many historical insights. These inscriptions might simply refer to some well known historical event, such as AEGYPTO CAPTA on coins of Augustus struck in the year 28 B.C., referring to the conquest of Egypt and the defeat of the armies of Mark Antony and Cleopatra, or of the inscription IVDAEA CAPTA on the coins of Vespasian struck in A.D. 71, commemorating the military victory which quelled the insurrection of the Jews in Judaea.

Inscriptions on the coins issued by the central Roman authority, or by the colonial and provincial authorities, often give evidence of the political pronouncements that the issuers wished to emphasize to the general public, somewhat in the nature of news bulletins or sometimes as propaganda announcements. These, along with counter stamping and validation of issues, or just the noting of the issuing mints, can open up broad avenues of historical research.

An interesting aspect of the numismatic study of the coinage issues of the Roman Empire is the presence of the many often very fine portrait illustrations of the imperial families. Regarding these efforts of the die engravers to capture the likeness of the subject individuals the natural question arises: " How accurately do these portraits faithfully correspond to the real life appearance of the individuals they purportedly represented ?" The technical steps involved in the final striking of a coin or medallion all offer challenges and the possible introduction of unintentional distortions.

Although at times Rome was the only Imperial mint striking all denominations of the regular Roman coinage, throughout the period under consideration here, many regional mints were authorized as Imperial mints to issue some if not all denominations. In addition, drachmas, didrachmas, and cistophori were also issued at "Asiatic" mints. Thus at various times, in addition to that at Rome, Imperial mints were established at over 30 sites from Britain, France, and Spain to Central Europe and the ancient Near East. The mostly bronze coins issued by the provincial authority for local use seldom have fine enough examples of portraiture to merit attention for present purposes.

    A natural question arises concerning the reference model of the imperial subjects that were copied by the die engravers (scalptores), whether at one of the mint work shops in Rome and more particularly at remote branches of the mint. As a reasonable speculation, one might suppose that the required reference models would be produced at the imperial court or wherever ready access to the members of the royal family was available. The earlier monetary issues, until about A.D. 200 almost all originated in work shops in Rome. Statuary busts of high style and realistic appearance would most likely be readily available for model purposes at these locations. Later period monetary issues began to involve mints at numerous locations, at first at a small number of unidentified sites. After about the middle of the third century A.D., mint marks appearing on coins clearly indicated that a wide spread network of mints were in use. The nature of the models distributed to the die engravers now had to be more numerous and required that they be distributed in a timely fashion. The simplest mechanism to adopt would have been to distribute coins and medallions struck at the principal mint. Whether this in fact this was the method employed is not known, although it is clear that another intermediary step had to be interposed between the original subject and the die engraver at the mint site. (It should be noted that the need for creating many dies at the mint itself is necessary because a die wears out after several hundred coins are struck with it. The exact number of coins struck from a particular obverse die depends on a number of factors: the minimum acceptable sharpness of the resulting coin image; the die material used, whether tempered bronze, iron, or steel; the die structure, whether a simple punch die with a flat or curved surface, a massive hinged die, particularly of a "box" form; etc..The obverse die, showing the portrait, is generally replaced more frequently than the reverse die. The subject matter shown on the reverse die while often coordinated with the principal mint in Rome might also be generated de novo at the local mint for local purposes.)

    Once the reference model is presented to the die engraver at the mint, his artistic and engraving skills are brought into play. All the steps along the way compound any artistic failure to produce an accurate likeness at the end. Although many other factors may play a role, it is possible that the high style and accuracy of depiction of portraits invariably appearing on coins struck at Rome prior to A.D. 200 is due to the quality of the models available to be copied and by the cordon of skilled die engravers gathered from all corners of the empire. As the number of mints spread to many distant locations, other than Rome, the models used for copying were one additional step further removed from reality and the skill of the die engravers were generally no match to those at Rome. Not unexpectedly, coin specimens appear with an increasing range in quality, until the time of the end of the dynasties of the house of Valentinian and Theodosius (the point in time when this study ends) when even the highest available styles, including medallion issues lack conveying a convincing sense of reality.

    A telling result follows from a quantitative analysis of the fraction of the entire offering of Roman coins, illustrated in sales and auction catalogs, which are of an artistic rendition meriting consideration as realistic portraits. When this fraction or index is computed emperor by emperor while advancing through the imperatorial period, a discernible time dependent feature appears. Prior to, and including the Augustan period this index is unsatisfyingly meager. From the time of Augustus through the house of Severus, the index is surprisingly high and more or less constant from one emperor to the next. From this point in time (circa A.D. 250) to the establishment of the Tetrarchy the index slowly decreases. A substantial drop in the index follows in the next two decades. The erosion in the index continues thereafter at a rapid pace, until by the reign of Arcadius and Honorius very little realistic portraiture is available. At about this time very stylized fullfaced portraiture appears to dominate the coin issues. These coins offer negligible clues as to the true likeness of the emperors purportedly being illustrated.

The selection of the fractional index based on catalog illustrations apart from being immediately relevant, also has a desirable built in bias to high light the best portrait renditions since the inclusion of photographic illustrations in catalogs is expensive and is only merited for "quality" coins.

As an avid collector of Roman Imperatorial coins and medallions this author was attracted early on to obtaining the specimens that appeared to render the most artistic portraits showing genuine character and personality. Many important collections were acquired using similar criteria. Such judgments guiding specimen selections might of course prove misleading with regard to their genuine accuracy with respect to the true likeness of the individual represented. However, it should be noted that even those specimens of much cruder rendition often, albeit in an exaggerated manner, caricature striking profile features found on the more artistic versions, much in the manner of present day drawings of "Hirschfeld's cartoon-like" depiction of notable individuals, which nonetheless offer immediate recognition. To cite one instance, excellent examples of this sort appear on coins of Mark Antony. In spite of exhibiting this type of variance all the coin portraits are recognizably those of Mark Antony. It is the fact that such collective depictions each offer evidence of the true likeness of the subject individual which forms the basis for the present work.

There are many excellent books consisting of enlarged photographic illustrations of Imperial portraiture appearing on coins and medallions, such as: Kurt Lange, "Charecterkopfe der Weltgeschicte", 1949; Frank, R. and Hirmer, M., "Romische Kaiserportrats im Munzbild" 1969; or Kent, J.P.C. and Max and Albert Himmer, "Roman Coins", 1978. They generally offer one, or at most very few, examples for the most prominent individuals from the beginning of the Roman Imperatorial period (roughly from the first half of the first century, B.C.) through the end of the Tetrarchy (roughly the end of the third century, A.D.) Mostly missing are illustrations of the emperors with much rarer coinage issues or of very short and fleeting reigns.

The standard reference catalogs, such as Henry Cohen, "Medailles Imperiales", 1880-92 (line drawings), Mattingly, H. and Sydenham, E. "Roman Imperial Coinage", 1923-67, and Mattingly, H. and Carson, R. "British Museum Catalog" 1923-62, are excellent references for coin and medallion types but offer very little in the way of good portraiture examples, except perhaps in quantity.

Frequently the auction catalogs and occasionally fixed price catalogs of the well known establishments have excellent photographs of coins and medallions, albeit usually in the small original size of the actual specimens. Occasionally, to show noteworthy detail, enlarged copies of the standard specimen sized photographs are also shown . As a small sample of the numerous catalogs in possession of the author found useful in this work, there are those of the Classical Numismatic Group, Adolph Hess and Bank Leu, Numismatic Fine Arts, Munzen und Medaillen, Schulman, Hirsch, Stack's, and Spink.

Comparing the best examples of imperial portraiture in available references raises the question, particularly with the lesser known emperors or those with only small coin issues, whether a method could be devised to give in some sense an "average" result over a number of exceptional selections rather than just selecting one "best" photographic example. This present work is in fact an attempt to obtain just such "averages". The resulting images are intended to give as true a portrait representation of the subject emperors as possible using only numismatic evidence. The present illustrations are the largest and most complete collection of quality portraits derived from coins of the Roman Imperatorial period.

In the method to be described below and the results shown, the various imperatorial figures, only material based on coins and medallions is used, deliberately avoiding any influence from photographs of statuary. The reasons for this are first of all, to avoid any error in identification of individuals and secondly, to be able, with the same technique, to generate results for those individuals for whom no statuary exists. It should be noted that original Roman statuary does not bear any identification of the individual represented. (It is alleged that saving of a magnificent equestrian statue of Marcus Aurelius from being melted down to provide bronze for casting cannons is due to a case of misidentification. The emperor is shown saluting his troops, a gesture misinterpreted to be the offering of a blessing, and the emperor himself being mistaken for Constantine, the first Christian emperor. This mistaken identification made the statue sacrosanct and inviolable to destruction, all because the Romans did not identify their statuary and memory recollection did not extend to the Italian Renaissance.)

The well known museum identified busts of notables, such as Augustus, Trajan, Hadrian etc. were all attributed based on comparisons with the portraiture appearing on coins and medallions and the copious identification included on all such specimens. When it comes to the identification of the distaff members of the imperial family, identification of statuary is even occasionally based on hair style comparisons with coin specimens.

There is of course, the need to eventually compare the presently obtained results with unambiguously identified sculpture. If such comparisons provide a close match, then it might be reasonable to suppose that the results presently obtained, that cannot be compared in this way, are also probably fairly accurate. Finally, it might be hoped that as yet unidentified statuary could also be reliably attributed.

It is most certainly true that for statuary that is indisputably identified, reference to these three dimensional works of art would be the best way to address the question, closely related to the present narrower objective, "What did these individuals look like in real life?" For practical reasons such viewing is best accomplished by a museum visit, at least while awaiting the availability of flat holographic pictures.

The source materials used in this study consist of photographs in the many catalogs in the authors possession, a few specimens of coins and medallions in his own collection, and over a dozen plaster casts of selected medallions in the British Museum, obtained through the kind courtesy offered the author by Dr. Carson, at the time curator of the Roman medallion collection.

For the imperatorial period up through the reign of Diocletian and in a few cases for later emperors, as many as four to six samples were selected for each imperatorial figure (each specimen dated to represent the individual at the same age). Exceptions, due to a lack of available examples of suitable quality, allowed for the use of only two examples to be selected in two cases (eg. two antoninianii for each of the usurpers Pacatian and Jotapian) and in one case only one example was found to be suitable (an aureus of Macrianus "II"). As stated earlier these selections were all examples judged superior in artistic rendition and exhibited lifelike character.

There follows a detailed description of the techniques used to obtain "average" portraitures for these cases where abundant realistic material was available. The paucity of good examples after the period of the Tetrachy, required a modification in methodology. This will be discussed later.

Several techniques were tried to obtain an image of a standard portrait size for each example (the overall bust illustration corresponds to approximately seven inches in height). The first step mostly consisted of taking a 35 mm. photograph, using a close-up lens attachment on the camera, so arranged as to fill the entire frame of the film with the image of the bust. An early procedure for obtaining final positive prints all of a single matched size for the portrait portion of the busts, used an enlarger with an adjustable magnification, following usual dark room methods. This technique gave excellent results, but was very time consuming. Several alternate procedures were tried, but all proved either cumbersome or equally time consuming. Finally, with the advent of computer managed image scanning, the presently used technique became possible. This approach is both rather rapid and very flexible in many respects.

Again, a 35 mm. image is obtained as before, the film however, is a standard "print" type. The film is commercially processed to give an ordinary 5x7 inch print. (The least expensive procedure is to use color film and a color enlarged print; using only black and white film is more expensive and commercial development takes longer! Incidentally, even high speed color film shows virtually no graininess.)

These photographically enlarged prints are then electronically scanned with a flatbed scanner (with a 1200 dpi resolution) resulting in a digital image under an ordinary PC computer control. This electronically recorded image can be easily enlarged to whatever size is required (magnifications in one percent steps are readily available in order to secure images of the same portrait size for any given emperor). In addition, manipulations such as inverting left-right, sharpening or averaging pixel resolution etc. are obtained with simple computer key strokes or mouse pointer commands. The acquired image is then printed out with an ink-jet printer with adjustable gray control (at this point a printer with a 300 dpi resolution is quite satisfactory) The final aim of this process to this point is to obtain separate individual prints of an emperor that in each case represents the best efforts of the involved die engraver.

The "averaging" process using these ink prints for a particular emperor is rather complicated, but simply unavoidable. Using translucent tracing paper a carefully rendered line drawing showing the principal features appearing on each separate print is obtained. Even though all these tracings (perhaps as many as six separate examples in some cases) are of the same portrait size, trying to obtain an average result for a particular emperor by simply overlaying them all, one on top of the other, (accomplished with the aid of a light box) could in principle produce a single average image, but proves to be in fact rather unsatisfactory. This is true no matter how the several tracings are indexed with respect to each other. Small changes in the relative size of facial features, or the angles of the forehead or the inclinations of the chin, differences in the relative overall size of the head with respect to the size of the frontal features, all add up to produce an unsatisfactory effect. However, this combined overlay can be used to the give the average location of principal portrait features relative to each other. Then, separate best <u>local</u> indexing of the overlays can be used to determine, for example, the shape of the nose to brow contour, yet another separately selected best local indexing of the overlays to determine the shape of the nose to chin contour, and separately indexed overlays to determine the best shape of the mouth, eyes etc. Based on such details a combined final overlaid "grand average" hand drawn portrait results. At this point shaded high lights are added to suggest surface modeling. It is evident that the authors artistic skill in addition to those of the die engravers has entered into producing the final outcome.

 An interesting finding developed in executing the above program. Denari were found to generally foreshorten the front to back dimension of the head in comparison to the length of the profile contour. This may probably have been done to allow the largest portion of the coin flan to be devoted to the more easily recognizable feature of the portrait. This type of distortion was not present with aurei even though the flan size of these coins is the same. The bronze coins did not appear to have this type of distortion either. Most of the individual examples used for source selections were of aurei, medallions, and a few large bronzes.

 The majority of imperial portraits appearing on coins and medallions are shown facing to the right. Occasionally, as for example, for the emperors Titus, Commodus, and Probus, to cite a few cases, coins and medallions exist showing some portraits facing to the right and some facing to the left. The scanning software capable of left-right inversion offered a ready means of the comparison for these cases. No discernible difference was found when comparisons were made . Perhaps this is not so surprising, since by its very nature the contour outline of a portrait in exact profile does not depend on whether it is a right or left handed view. The quite general asymmetry of the left and right side of the face would only show up in the facial modelling of the portrait. Even for the asymmetric appearance of a scowling Caracalla this difference would be hard to capture for a die engraver resulting in any substantial difference between the left and right handed views. In any event , the averaging overlays used in the present analysis mostly involve individual portraits facing in the same direction.

 The procedure for generating realistic and believable portraits for the imperatorial figures reigning after the Tetrarchy possesses serious problems, making the above described methodology inapplicable and even suspect if applied. Either only one credible sample was found for a particular individual, or when a few possibilities existed the disparity between choices was so great that no believable overlay procedure could be trusted.

Instead, in each case the "best possible" example was enlarged to the adopted standard size using the electronic devises previously described. Employing the artistic skill of the author this resulting portrait was then modified, to include at least to some extent, any idiosyncratic portrait features appearing in other possible choices that were however, judged less overall appealing.

The copies of the finished drawings of the Imperatorial portraits are presented in the following pages of this work. Because of the artistic intervention of the author, particularly for the late emperors, the portraits are in fact most properly described as "based" on Roman Imperatorial coinage and medallions. In no case, however, are they simply mechanically rendered copies of any single sample no matter how attractive a specimen it might be. A number of specimens were always involved in generating the final result. The author believes that the assembled portrait likenesses in this work should eventually be compared with statuary, a project now under consideration.

A brief identification of each individual is given. Some biographical information is also included to help place the individuals in a historical context and to define their personalities. These brief commentaries are not intended to chronicle the historical scene in any detail. The years specified by the designation " reigned " for each imperial figure is the time span of all imperial titles and powers, whether granted by the Senate, or army legions. Where appropriate, the periods of acclamation as Caesar and Augustus are separately cited.

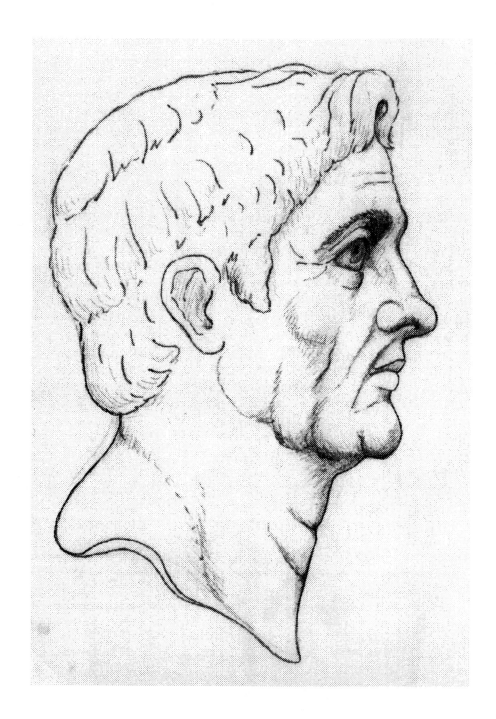

"POMPEY, the GREAT"
(*Cnaeus Pompeius Magnus*)

Born 106 B.C.   Imperator and Consul 83 - 48 B.C.   Died 48 B.C.

His valor and success in brilliant military and naval actions gained him many triumphal honors. He was awarded the title of Magnus (the Great) for these splendid exploits. In 60 B.C., he joined with Caesar and Crassus, to form the First Triumvirate. Quarreling with Caesar led to his defeat at Pharsalia. Escaping to Egypt he was murdered on his arrival there in 48 B.C.

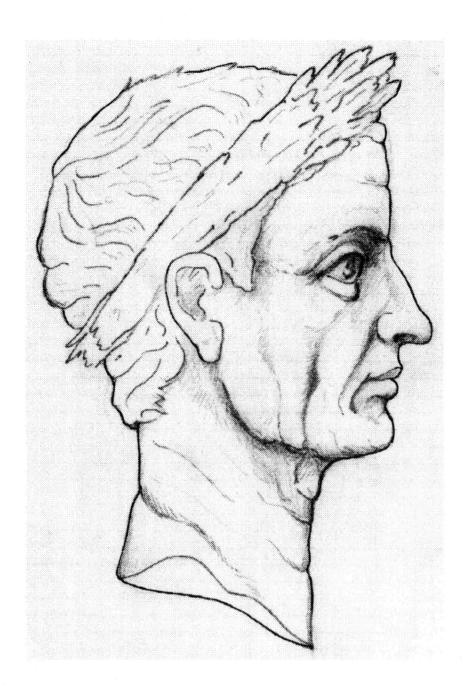

" JULIUS CAESAR "
(*Caius Julius Caesar*)

Born 100 B.C.　　　Reigned approximately 59 B.C.- 44 B.C.　　　Died 44 B.C.

  He was conferred as Consul in 59 B.C., after forming the First Triumvirate with Pompey the Great and Crassus. A fallout over interests with Pompey led to the defeat of the latter at Pharsalia in 48 B.C. As a great commander with many military successes he was elevated by the Senate to increasing personal authority in Rome. Eventually, this led to his assassination on the Ides of March, 44 B.C.

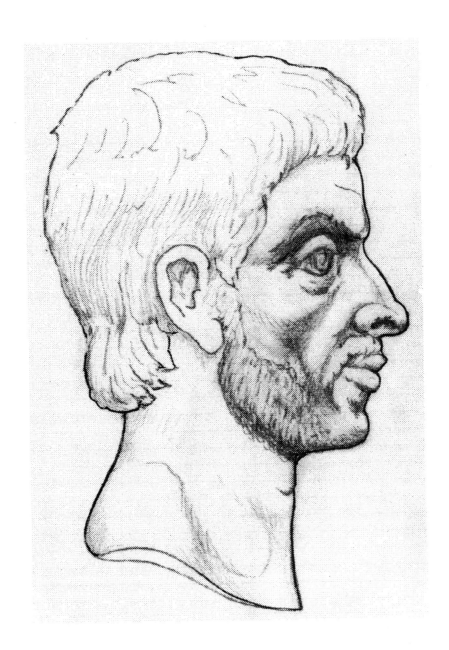

" BRUTUS "
(Marcus Junius Brutus)

Born 85 B.C.   Died 42 B.C.

He supported Pompey in the civil wars against Julius Caesar. After the defeat of Pompey at Pharsalia Brutus was pardoned by Caesar. He rewarded Caesar by joining the conspiracy that led to the assassination of Caesar on the Ides of March 44 B.C. Mark Antony and Octavian defeated the joint forces of Brutus and Cassius at Philippi on 42 B.C. Brutus died by his own hand upon this defeat.

"AHENOBARBUS"
(*Cneus Domitius Ahenobarbus*)

Born ?   Died ca. 28 B.C.

He was a descendent of the famous and distinguished Domiti family. First, he found favor with Julius Caesar, after whose death he allied himself with Brutus, one of Caesar's assassins. During the land battle, in 42 B.C. at Philippi, when Brutus and Cassius were defeated by Mark Antony and Octavian (Augustus), Ahenobarbus having been placed in command of a powerful fleet by Brutus' party, won an impressive victory fought on the Ionian Sea, for which he was awarded the title " Imperator ". He also successfully blockaded the Roman ports on the Ionian coast. He was reconciled with Mark Antony after the death of Brutus and Cassius, who then made him governor of Bithynia. However, shortly before the battle of Actium he deserted to Octavian.

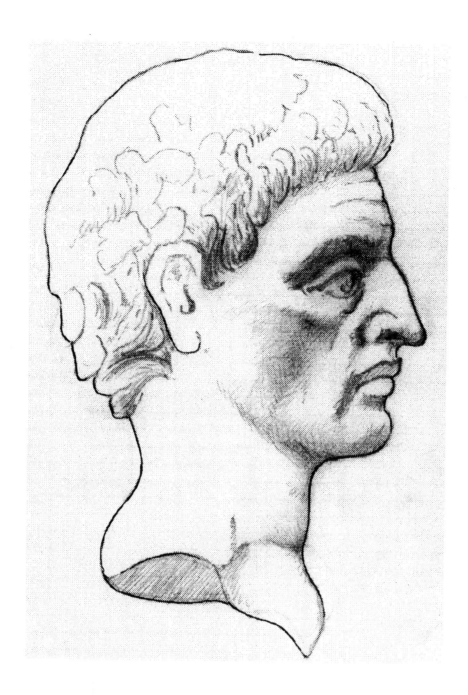

"LABIENUS"
(*Quintus Labienus*)

Born ?   Died 39 B.C.

A Roman general under the Republic, he later joined forces with Brutus. He was dispatched to Parthia in 44 B.C. to seek help from that regions king Orodes, who had previously sided with Pompey against Caesar, and who cast his lot with Brutus. The Parthian auxiliaries led by Labienus and Pacorus, the son of Orodes, were defeated by Ventidius Bassus, the Roman general in Syria in 39 B.C.

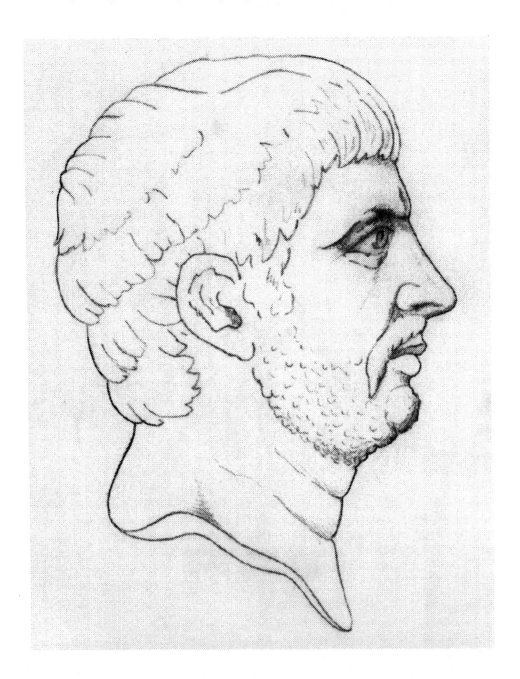

" SEXTUS POMPEY "
(*Sextus Pompeius Magnus*)

Born 65 B.C.   Died 35 B.C.

Sextus Pompeius, brother of Pompeius Cnaeius, was the youngest son of Pompey the Great. Sextus assumed his father's title "Magnus" as a hereditary right. The two brothers fought Caesar to avenge their father's death, and were completely defeated at Munda, in Spain, in 45 B.C. Sextus barely escaped, Cnaeius having been killed in battle. After Caesar's death, Sextus assembled a great naval fleet and dominated the Mediterranean Sea, seizing Sicily as his base. Octavian sent Agrippa, at the head of a powerful navy against Sextus. Sextus was totally defeated and fled to Phrygia where he was captured by Mark Antony's officers who beheaded him in 35 B.C.

"CLEOPATRA"
(Cleopatra VII ?)

Born 69 B.C.   Queen of Egypt 42 - 30 B.C.   Died 30 B.C.

   Cleopatra was the daughter of Ptolemy XII (Auletes) and last Dynastic Queen of Egypt. Upon the elimination of rival siblings, she became sole ruler of Egypt in 42 B.C. She is noted for having had a lustful relationship with both Julius Caesar and Mark Antony. She had a son by Caesar and three children by Mark Antony. This talented sovereign princess was an ambitious and accomplished diplomatic player on the Roman world stage. This portrait of Cleopatra is largely based on coinage struck in Alexandria showing her at an age between 18 and 24 years.

" CLEOPATRA "

Cleopatra's ambition to rule with Mark Antony as Queen of Kings was shattered with the defeat of Mark Antony by Augustus at Actium in 31 B.C. She committed suicide the following year in 30 B.C. Her portrait here is at an age between 30 to 39 years, as depicted on many coins, mostly struck conjugate with the bust of Mark Antony on the other side.

"MARK ANTONY"
(*Marcus Antonius*)

Born 83 B.C.   Died 30 B.C.

He was created Tribune in 50 B.C. at age 34. The following year he threw his lot in with Julius Caesar, campaigning with him as a cavalry commander in Gaul and Pharsalia, he also lent military support to Caesar in Egypt and Asia. In 43 B.C., after the assassination of Caesar he formed a contentiously brokered Second Triumvirate with Octavian (later called Augustus), his principal rival for the domination of Rome, with Lepidus in a lesser role. In 42 B.C. allied with Octavian, he defeated Brutus and Cassius, the principal assassins of Caesar, at Philippi. In 41 B.C. while campaigning in Greece, Cappadocia, and Cilicia he met Cleopatra in Tarsus. He joined her in Alexandria in a tragic liaison. Quarrels with Octavian ruptured the triumvirate, and Mark Antony was vanquished in the battle of Actium in 31 B.C. He fled with Cleopatra to Alexandria. Anticipating total defeat he died by his own sword in 30 B.C.

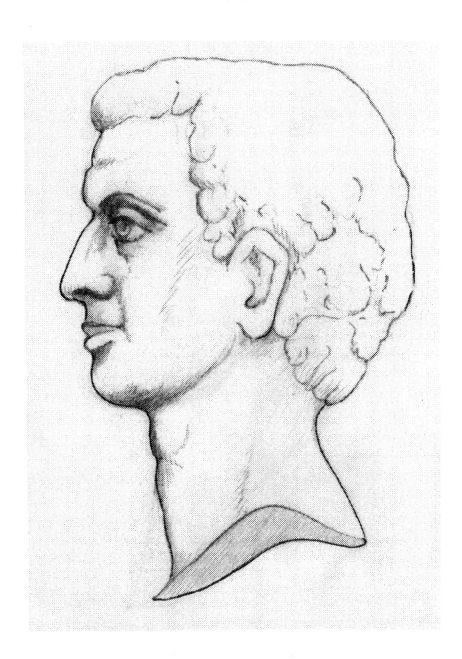

"LEPIDUS"
(*Marcus Aemilius Lepidus*)

Born ?   Died 13 B.C.

A follower of Julius Caesar and his colleague in the Consulateship in the year 46 B.C., Lepidus was a minor partner in the Second Triumvirate with Mark Antony and Octavian (Augustus) in 43 B.C. The Triumvirs divided the Roman provinces, and the Western provinces fell to Octavian, the Eastern to Mark Antony, and Spain and Gallia Narbonensis to Lepidus. Overreaching his authority, Lepidus failed in his efforts to acquire Sicily for himself and was stripped of all authority except that of Pontifex Maximus. He passed the remainder of his life in retired obscurity.

" OCTAVIA "
(*Octavia*)

Born 62 B.C.   Died 11 B.C.

  She was the sister of Octavian (Augustus). To cement ties between Mark Antony and Octavian, the two principal Triumvirs, Octavia was married to Mark Antony in 40 B.C. She was his second wife. Mark Antony divorced her in 32 B.C. having left her for Cleopatra. She died about 20 years later, a grieving mother for her dead son Marcellus.

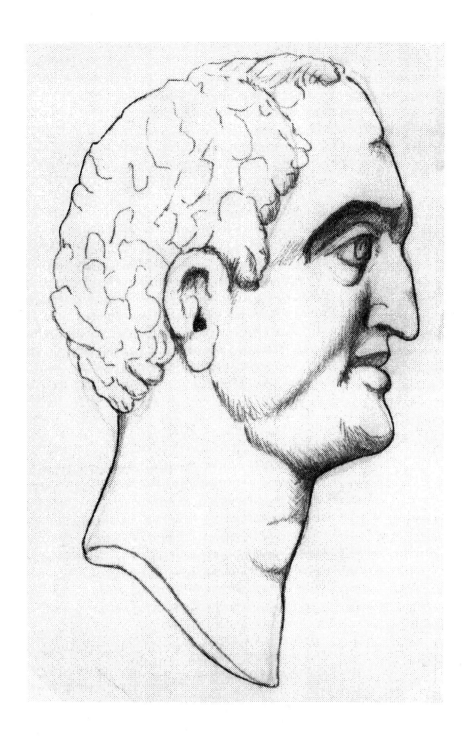

" LUCIUS ANTONIUS "
(*Lucius Antonius*)

Born ?   Died ?

He was the brother of Mark Antony. In 41 B.C. Lucius Antonius was made Consul. He instigated the Persian Wars against Octavian and was defeated and captured. Pardoned by Octavian, he was given the governorship of Spain.

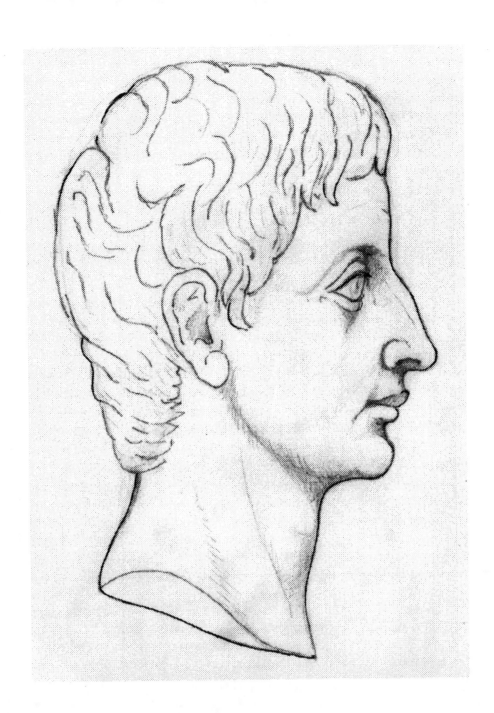

" AUGUSTUS "
(*Caius Julius Caesar Octavianus*)

Born 63 B.C.   Reigned 27 B.C. - A.D. 14   Died A.D. 14

Originally named Caius Octavius Thurinus, he became the adopted son of Julius Caesar. Octavian, now renamed, formed the Second Triumvirate in 43 B.C. with Mark Antony and Lepidus after the assassination of Julius Caesar. Soon quarrels errupted with Mark Antony. After the defeat of Mark Antony at Actium in 31 B.C. he ruled as sole master of Rome. He was designated Augustus in 27 B.C. During his entire long reign, he continued to be depicted on his contemporary coins to be at a more or less constant age of 30 - 35.

" AUGUSTUS "

Commemorative or restitution coins struck after the death of Augustus were issued by numerous emperors from Tiberius to Trajan Decius. Possibly these, all showing Augustus appearing to be at a more advanced age, were based on contemporary statuary existing on his estate. In this example he is shown to be at an age of 45 - 50. Coins of this type are all shown radiate and usually facing to the left.

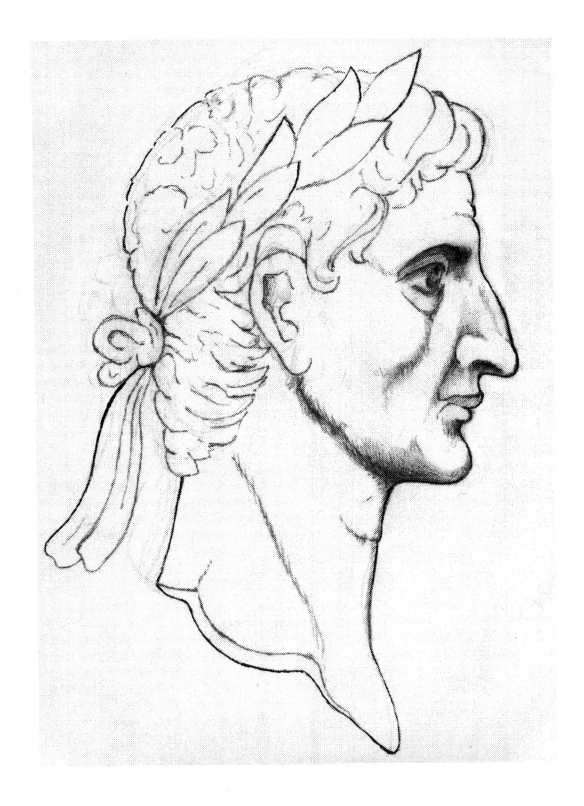

" AUGUSTUS "

This portrait is based on restitution coins showing a rather aged Augustus, perhaps 70 years or older. These coins generally show a bare headed or laueate profile facing to the right. It is said of him " he found a Rome of bricks and left it of marble ".

"LIVIA"
(*Livia Drusilla*)

Born 56 B.C.   Died A.D. 29

She was the wife of Tiberius Claudius Nero who was forced to yield her to become the fourth wife of Augustus in 38 B.C. She bore two sons, Tiberius and Nero Drusus, by the earlier marriage. She may have been implicated in the deaths of possible heirs of Augustus, and finally Augustus himself, presumably to advance the fortunes of her son Tiberius. No coins of Livia were struck during the entire long reign of Augustus. The first definitive portrait coins were issued by Tiberius, in approximately A.D. 22 - 23. The portrait shown here is of that period and shows her at an age clearly younger than the 78 - 79 years that would correspond to the year of this issue. Perhaps this portrait is modelled after earlier statuary found on the estate of Augustus.

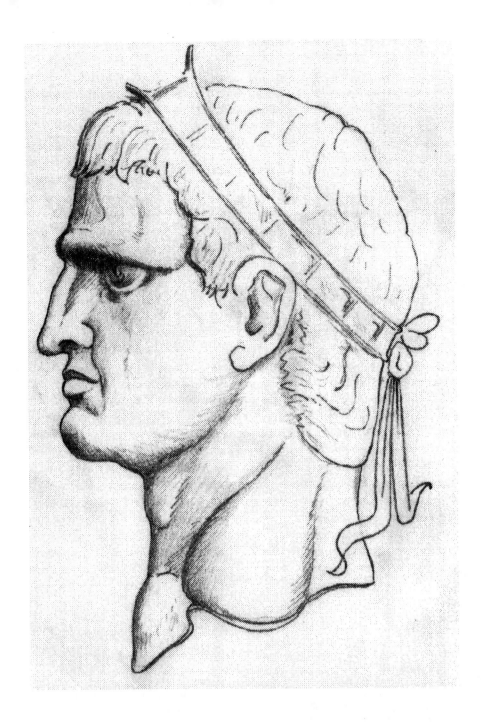

"AGRIPPA"
(*Marcus Vipsanius Agrippa*)

Born 63 B.C.   Died 12 B.C.

He was a renowned commander, both by sea and land and the son-in-law of Octavian, having married his daughter Julia in 21 B.C. Agrippa at the head of a Roman fleet was dispatched by Octavian (Augustus) to depose Sextus Pompey in Sicily, who he easily defeated. He shared in the victory at Philippi and helped in the defeat of Mark Antony at Actium. Agrippa was designated by Augustus as his successor but predeceased the emperor in 12 B.C.

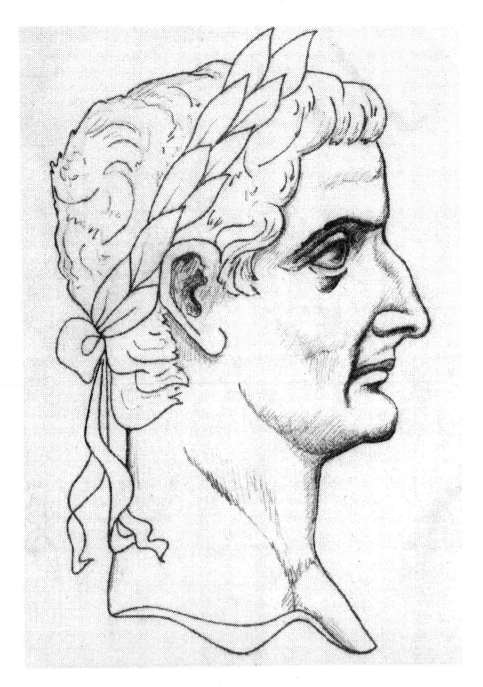

"TIBERIUS"
(Tiberius Claudius Nero)

Born 42 B.C.   Reigned A.D. 14 - 37   Died A.D. 37

He was the son of Tiberius Claudius Nero, a member of the distinguished Claudian line, and Livia and after the marriage of Livia to Octavian (Augustus) he became his stepson and eventually his adopted son after the death of Agrippa in A.D. 12. Augustus conferred upon Tiberius many important commands at the border regions of the Roman empire. Of these assignments he acquitted himself with great distinction. He succeeded Augustus as emperor A.D. 14 at the age of 55. Although an able administrator he became increasingly cruel and fond of vile debaucheries. With the aid of Sejanus, his praetorian commander, there were many " treason trials " and much blood letting, leading to a general disgust for the emperor. He died in A.D. 37 during a long odious seclusion on the isle of Capreae.

"DRUSUS, junior"
(Nero Claudius Drusus)

Born ca. 15 B.C.   Died A.D. 23

Drusus "junior" was the son of Tiberius by his first wife Vipsania Agrippina. He was an able soldier but of shallow character. In spite of his character flaws he advanced through many public honors, including Questor and twice Consul. An heir apparent to the throne after the death of Germanicus, he was poisoned by his wife Livilla under the influence of the praetorian commander Sejanus in A.D. 23. They were exposed by Apicata, the wife of Sejanus in a letter to Tiberius some eight years after the event. Coins showing Drusus at an age of about 35 were struck just prior to his death. The same bust also appears on restitution coins struck under Titus.

"DRUSUS, senior"
(*Nero Claudius Drusus*)

Born 38 B.C.   Died 9 B.C.

  Drusus "senior" was the younger brother of Tiberius, the son of Livia and her first husband Ti. Claudius Nero. With the consent of her husband, Livia later married Octavian (Augustus). Drusus married Antonia, the daughter of Mark Antony, and was the father of Germanicus and Claudius the future emperor. He died from wounds inflicted when he was thrown by his horse on the journey home from the Rhine frontier. His coins are all restoration issues struck under Claudius and later emperors.

"ANTONIA"
(*Antonia*)

Born ca. 38 B.C.   Died A.D. 38

Antonia was the daughter of Mark Antony and Octavia. She was married to Drusus senior ca. 16 B.C., and was the mother of Germanicus, Livilla, and the afterwards emperor Cladius.

"GERMANICUS"
(*Germanicus*)

Born 15 B.C.   Died A.D. 19

He was the son of Drusus senior, and Antonia. He was also the nephew of Tiberius who adopted him in A.D. 14 at the insistence of Augustus. For his military exploits in the German Wars he was awarded a splendid triumph on his return to Rome in A.D. 17. Dispatched to the East, where he gained considerable military and diplomatic successes he died mysteriously in A.D. 19. It seems probable that he was poisoned by Piso, prefect of Syria, and his wife Plancia, with the approval of Tiberius and Livia.

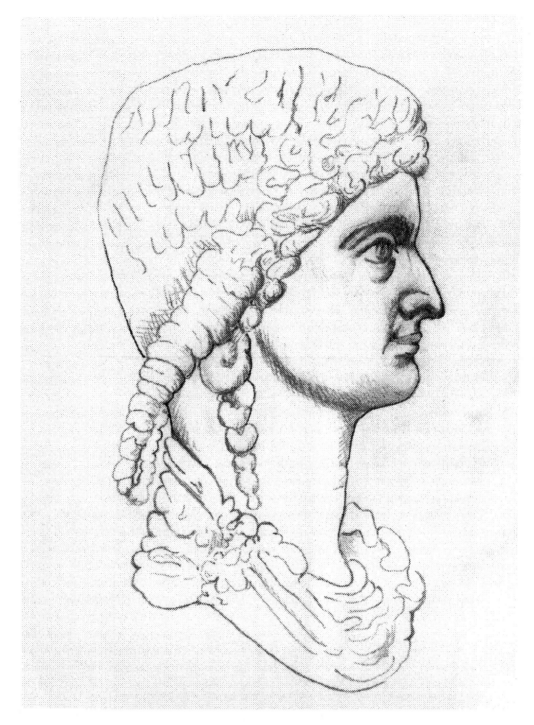

" AGRIPPINA, senior "
(*Agrippina*)

Born 15 B.C.   Died A.D. 33

  She was the daughter of Agrippa and Julia, the daughter of Augustus. She married Germanicus ca. A.D. 5 and was the mother of emperor Caligula. She accompanied her husband Germanicus to Syria only to see him poisoned by the agents of Tiberius. She brought his ashes back to Rome amidst great lamenting by the soldiers and the populace. First just persecuted by Tiberius, he finally accused her of treason and banished her to the island of Pandatonia in A.D. 29, where on his orders she was starved to death in A.D. 33. All coins showing her portrait where struck after her death.

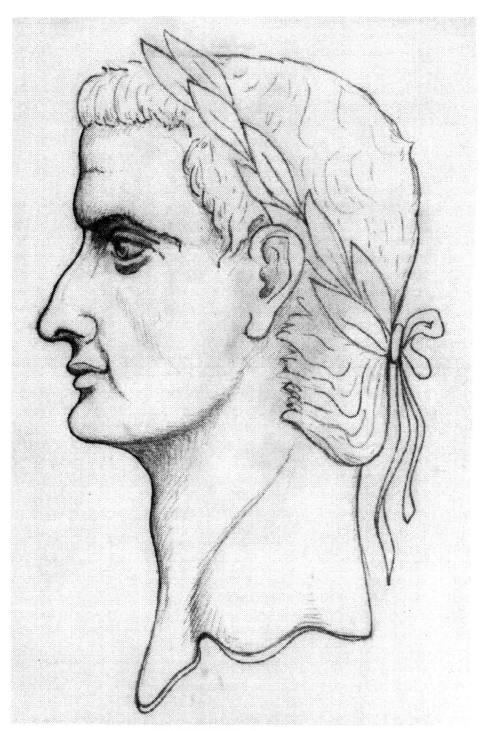

"CALIGULA"
(*Caius Caesar*)

Born A.D. 12   Reigned A.D. 37-41   Died A.D. 41

He was the son of Germanicus and Agrippina "senior". The name "Caligula" derives from a nickname given him by the soldiers meaning "little boot", referring to his fondness as a child for wearing footgear, called Caliga in camp. Under the influence of his grandmother Antonia he initiated his reign as emperor with great promise. Recovering from a serious illness he progressively became more depraved and cruel. The excessively luxurious imperial court life style and extravagant spectacles soon exhausted the huge treasury bestowed on him by Tiberius and led to a reign of terror involving the slaughter of wealthy citizens and seizing of their treasure. He was assassinated in a senatorial plot in A.D. 41.

"CLAUDIUS"
(*Tiberius Claudius Drusus*)

Born 10 B.C.　　　　　　Reigned A.D. 41 - 54　　　　　　Died A.D. 54

Perceived as a dullard, he was largely ignored by the imperial family. Upon the death of his nephew Caligula in A.D. 42, he was proclaimed emperor by the Pretorian Guard. He began the long occupation of Britain by his conquest of the island in A.D. 43. He had his unfaithful wife Messalina and her paramour C.Silius put to death. A year later in A.D.49 he married his niece Agrippina. Due to her influence Claudius designated her son Nero as heir to the throne, bypassing Britannicus who was his son with Messalina. Claudius died in A.D. 54 under suspicion that he was poisoned by Agrippina.

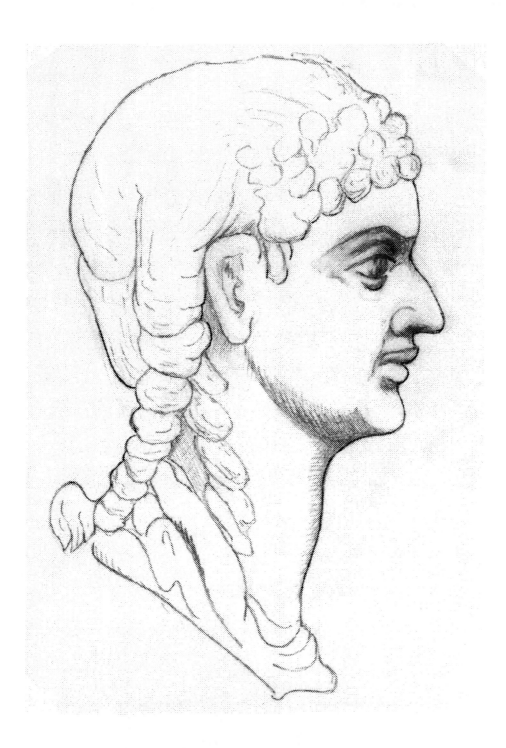

"AGRIPPINA, junior"
(*Agrippina Julia*)

Born 16   Died 59

She was the sister of Caligula and niece of Claudius, whom she married in the year 49 becoming his second wife. She is reported to have been a great beauty. She had a son, Nero, by a previous marriage to the senator Cn. Domitius Ahenobarbus. She is implicated in the death of Claudius, aided by Locusta, a sorceress well versed in the poisoning arts. Agrippina was put to death by her ungrateful son Nero in the year 59.

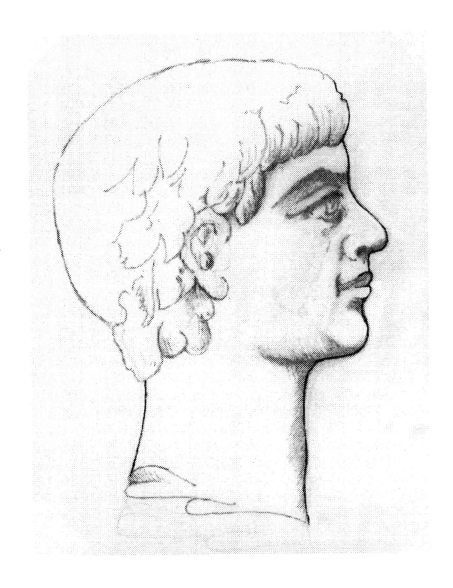

" BRITANNICUS "
(Tiberius Claudius Germanicus)

Born 42   Died 55

The son of Claudius by his first marriage to Messalina, he was renamed Ti. Claudius Britannicus to commemorate the conquest of Britain by Claudius. Through the influence of Agrippina, the second wife of Claudius, he was deprived of his right as heir to the throne. Instead, Agrippina's son Nero was proclaimed heir in the year 50. Nero had Britannicus poisoned in the year 55.

"NERO"
(*Nero Claudius Caesar Drusus Germanicus*)

Born 37 Reigned 54-68 Died 68

He was the son of Cn. Domitius Ahenobarbus and Agrippina "junior". Agrippina after marrying the emperor Claudius in 49, induced him to adopt Nero and proclaim him heir to the throne, thereby forsaking his own son Britannicus born to Claudius and his previous wife Messalina. After the death of Caudius in 54, possibly aided to his demise with poison administered by Agrippina, Nero became emperor. In 55, Britannicus an ever present challenger to the throne was poisoned. Guided by Seneca and Burrus, Nero at first was a model ruler. He was an enthusiastic devotee of the arts. The present portrait depicts Nero in his teens.

"NERO"

After the death of Burrus in 62 and the retirement of Seneca, Nero threw all restraint to the wind and embarked on a career of extravagance and cruelty. He had his mother Agrippina murdered in 59. He engaged in various vile sexual practices and justifiably became most unpopular, especially when it was rumored that he caused the great fire which destroyed half of the city of Rome in 64. His extravagant new "Golden House", was built on the land cleared after the fire. The infamous Nero died by a forced suicide at the age of only 30 in 68. The present portrait is at his age of about 25.

" GALBA "
(*Servius Sulpicius Galba*)

Born 3 B.C.　　　　　Reigned A.D. 68 - 69　　　　　Died A.D. 69

   Galba held several positions of public office including the appointment by Nero to jurisdiction of Hispania Tarraconensis in A.D. 60. After Nero's death he was proclaimed emperor by his troops. His neglect of public affairs together with his estrangement from the army led to his assassination after having reigned for only seven months. The year A.D. 69 saw four different emperors reign with Galba as first, followed by Otho, Vitellius, and Vespasian.

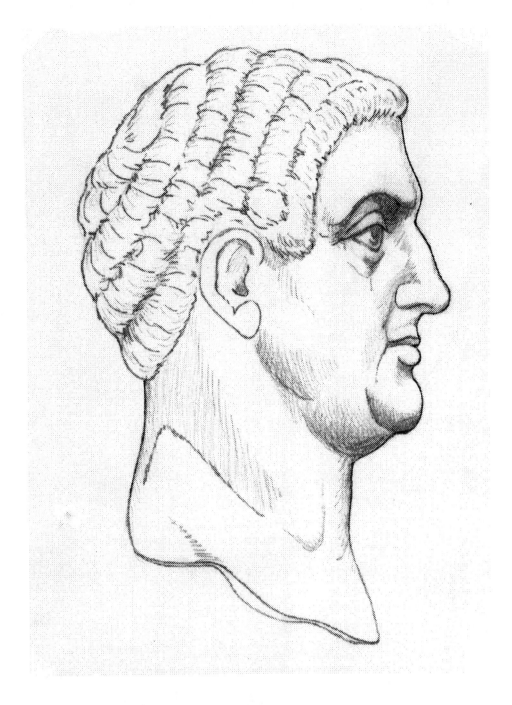

" OTHO "
(*Marcus Salvius Otho*)

Born 32 Reigned 69 Died 69

He was a favorite of Nero and adopted his excessive debaucheries. He is said to have depilated his whole body and wore an ill fitting wig as shown here. He conspired with Galba in a plot which led to Nero's death. Feeling betrayed when Galba as emperor, did not declare him heir to the throne, he set about to instigate a praetorian assassination of Galba. Declared emperor by the praetorian guard he was immediately forced to face Vitellius also declared emperor by his own troops in Germany. Otho's forces were completely defeated and he deliberately slew himself by his own hands. His reign lasted but 95 days.

" VITELLIUS "
(Aulus Vitellius Germanicus)

Born A.D. 14   Reigned 69   Died 69

  As a youth he lived at Capreae with Tiberius and was a favorite with the emperors Caligula, Claudius, and Nero. In the year 68 the emperor Galba unwisely appointed him as commander of the legions in Germany. Vitellius was soon declared emperor by his troops in a revolt against Galba. Meanwhile, Otho was declared emperor upon the assassination of Galba. Otho mounted a campaign in northern Italy to intercept Vitellius on his march on Rome. Otho's forces were defeated and Vitellius became sole ruler of the Empire. He enjoyed the imperial power for only 8 months after a rampage of gluttony and deviant sex practices. The soldiers of the challenger Vespasian captured Vitellius who died an inglorious death, his body having been dragged through the streets of Rome and thrown into the Tiber.

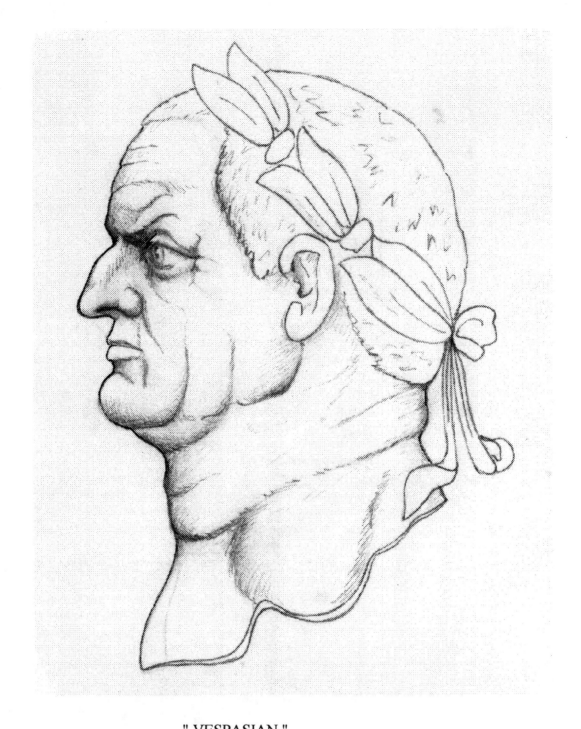

" VESPASIAN "
(Titus Flavius Sabinus Vespasianus)

Born A.D. 9   Reigned 69-79   Died 79

The first of the Flavian emperors, he was the son of Flavius Sabinus and Vespasia Polla. He was an able soldier of middle class origins and with a first hand knowledge of every corner of the Empire, having also accompanied Claudius on the conquest of Britian and the quieting of the Jewish rebellion. The Alexandrian and Danubean legions declared for Vespasian as emperor. The forces of Vitellius were successfully defeated at Cremona and with Otho dead, Vespasian assumed complete power. He was a conscientious and efficient ruler and refreshingly unassuming. He built many splendid buildings and temples, including the famous Coloseum. Taken ill he died relatively peacefully in 79 at an age of 69.

"DOMITILLA"
(*Flavius Domitilla*)

Born ?   Died ca. A.D. 67

She was the first wife of Vespasian. They were married in A.D. 39 and she was the mother of the future emperors Titus and Domitian. She died before Vespasian became emperor. All coins referring to her were struck posthumously under emperor Titus.

"TITUS"
(*Titus Flavius Vespasianus*)

Born A.D. 4   Reigned 79-81   Died 81

He was the son of Vespasian and Flavia Domitilla. He received court education under emperor Claudius and had an early military career stationed in Germany and Britain. Titus accompanied his father on the military expedition, begun in A.D. 66, to subdue the Jewish uprising in Judaea. Vespasian having been declared emperor in A.D. 69 left Titus to complete the subjugation of Judaea, which he rapidly concluded with the capture of Jerusalem the following year. Actually, the fortress of Masada did not fall until A.D. 74. The year 69 was also a portentous year for Titus with the conquest of Britain by his general Agricola, the eruption of Mt. Vesuvius burying Pompeii and Herculaneum, and a destructive fire in Rome in a large area of the Capitol to the Pantheon. His generous relief aid in these catastrophes won him great popular acclaim. He died unexpectedly from an uncertain illness in the year 81.

"JULIA TITI"
(*Julia Titi*)

Born ? Died ?

She was the daughter of Titus by Furnilla, his second wife. It is alleged that Domitian fell in love with her and installed her as his mistress. She died in an attempt to rid herself of the resulting pregnancy.

"DOMITIAN"
(*Titus Flavius Domitianus*)

Born 51   Reigned 81-96   Died 96

He was the youngest son of Vespasian and the brother of Titus, with both of whom he had strained relations. He was declared emperor by the praetorian guard upon the death of childless Titus. He ruled autocratically, largely ignoring the Senate. He was an able administrator amidst a torrent of plots and conspiracies against his person. These incidents led to a violent reaction consisting of exaggerated paranoia driving the last years of his reign to one of terror and oppression. He was murdered in a palace plot involving his wife Domitia in 96.

" DOMITIA "
(*Domitia Longina*)

Born ?   Died ?

Domitia was married to the emperor Domitian in 82, later divorced on charges of adultery and remarried to him again to satisfy public demand. She was involved in the conspiracy to murder Domitian. After Domitian's assassination she retired to private life and died during the reign of Trajan.

"NERVA"
(*Marcus Cocceius Nerva*)

Born 32   Reigned 96-98   Died 98

He was on good terms with Nero, and the son of a wealthy lawyer. In 71 he was declared Consul and then colleague with Vespasian and later with Domitian. Upon the death of Domitian, the by now elderly, Nerva was declared emperor by the Senate and the Praetorians. He was a benevolent ruler and worked to improve the condition of the state. Failing to be popular with the army and having lost their support he placated them by adopting Trajan and designating him heir to the throne. Having reigned 16 months he died of natural causes. He ushered in an 80 year span of worthy and noble emperors.

"TRAJAN"
(*Marcus Ulpius Traianus*)

Born 52 Reigned 98-117 Died 117

Of Spanish birth, he held important military posts and was elevated to the rank of Consul in 91. He was adopted as heir to the throne by Nerva, just before the death of the latter in 97. As emperor he conducted successful military campaigns in Dacia and Parthia. With the addition of his military conquests the Roman Empire achieved the greatest extension of its boundaries. He attended to the construction of the Roman infrastructure and of public works. He was generally popular and admired as a just and natural leader. Trajan's portrait on his coins show very little aging, here he is shown at an approximate age of 55.

"PLOTINA"
(Pompeia Plotina)

Born ca. 70   Died 123

  She married Trajan sometime before his adoption by Nerva. They were childless and late in Trajan's reign she persuaded him to adopt Hadrian, her favorite in the court. She was a dignified and intellectual woman who was the trusted counselor of her husband throughout his reign. She was awarded the title "Augusta" in 105 acknowledging her virtuous character.

" MARCIANA "
(*Ulpia Marciana*)

born ? Died 114

Marciana was the sister of Trajan and the mother of Matidia. She lived as a widow with Trajan's wife Plotina in a harmonious relationship.

" MATIDIA "
(*Matidia*)

Born ? Died ?

Matidia was the daughter of Marciana, the niece of Trajan and the mother of Sabina who became the wife of Hadrian. Matidia was a virtuous woman following in her mother's footsteps. In the year 113 she was declared "Augusta" by decree of the Senate.

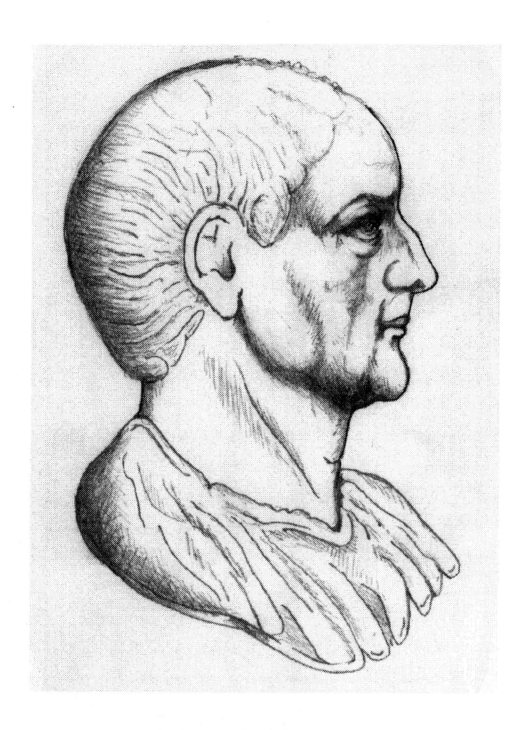

" TRAJAN, PATER "
(Marcus Ulpius Traianus)

Born ?   Died ca. 100

He was the emperor Trajan's father who had a distinguished civil and military career. He was the commander of the tenth legion during the Jewish War in 67-68, Consul around 70, and governor of Syria, later of Asia, and at one time the governor of a Spanish province.

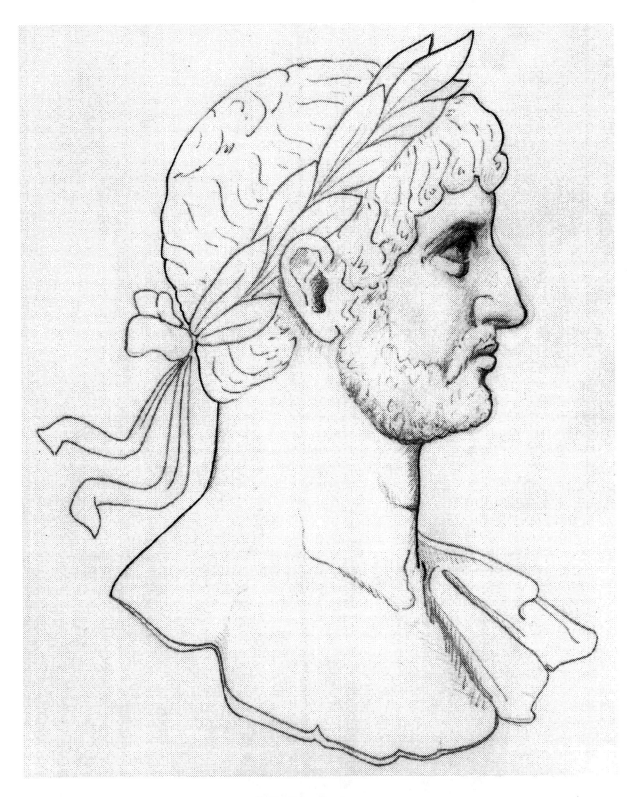

"HADRIAN"
(*Publius Aelius Hadrianus*)

Born 76 Reigned 117-138 Died 138

Losing his father as a youth of age 10, he was placed under the guardianship of Trajan, who appointed him to many high public positions of honor prior to his reaching the age of 40 years. In the year 117 he was adopted by Trajan just before that emperor's death, with the aid and support of the empress Plotina. It was said that he was " a man of culture and the arts rather than war ". He is shown here at an age of about 40.

" HADRIAN "

In many respects Hadrian was an ideal ruler, devoting most of his long reign to visiting all the provinces of the Roman Empire and generally improving the affairs of state. His first extended trip was to Britain, Gaul, and Spain in 121-123. While in Britain he ordered the construction of "Hadrian's Wall" in the North to provide a shield against the barbarians and protect the Roman provinces of Britain. He is shown here at the probable age of 47.

"HADRIAN"

Hadrian's extended trip to Carthage and North Africa occurred in 128 and followed quickly in 128-132 by trips to Greece, Ephesus, Jerusalem, and Alexandria. Here he is shown at the probable age of 53-55.

"HADRIAN"

Hadrian's final extended journey again took him to the Near East in 132-134. He planned to rebuild Jerusalem as a new Graeco-Roman city to be called Aelia Capitolina. In this portrait he is shown at the probable age of 60-62, corresponding to his age near the end of his reign.

"SABINA"
(*Vibia Sabina*)

Born ?   Died 136

Sabina was the daughter of Trajan's grand niece Matidia. Under the influence of Plotina she was married to Hadrian in the year 100. The marriage was extremely uncongenial and she was poorly treated by Hadrian. Part of the discord was Hadrian's homosexual preference shown for the Greek youth Antinous. Sabina committed suicide or was poisoned by Hadrian in 136.

" ANTINOUS "
(*Antinous*)

Born ?   Died 130

   This Bithynian youth was Hadrian's homosexual favorite. He accompanied Hadrian on his tours of the Empire. He accidentally drowned in the Nile during Hadrian's visit to Egypt. Shrines and temples were dedicated in his memory by the grieving emperor. Coins and medallions of Antinous appear only with Greek inscriptions, none in Latin.

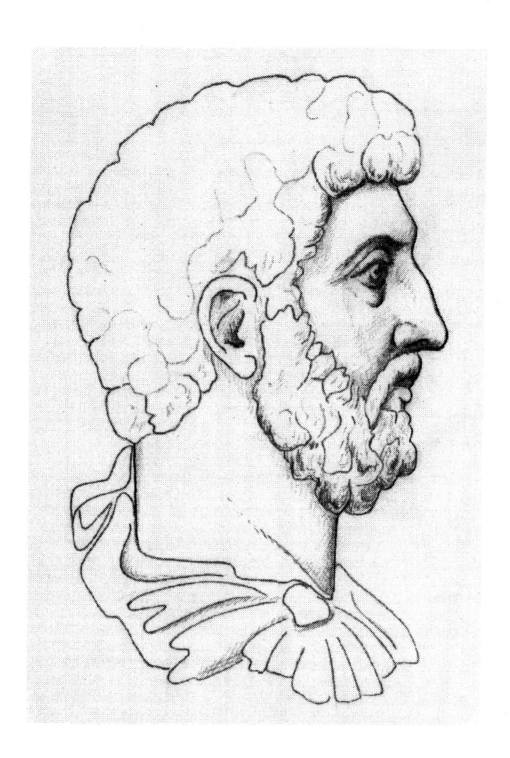

"AELIUS"
(*Lucius Ceionus Commodus*)

Born ? Reigned as Caesar 136-138 Died 138

Upon the death of Sabina, he was adopted as Lucius Aelius Verus Caesar by Hadrian in 136 as heir to the throne. He was learned, eloquent, and handsome. He was made Tribune, later Consul twice, and appointed prefect of Pannonia, where he governed with some skill. He predeceased Hadrian in 138, dying of tuberculosis.

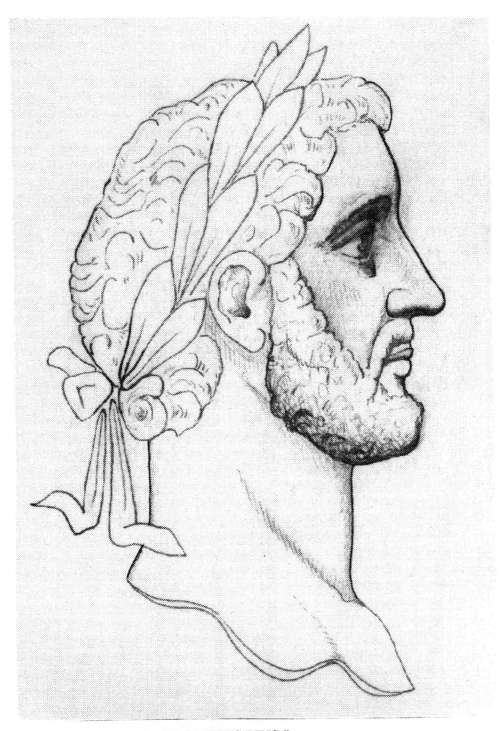

" ANTONINUS PIUS "
(Titus Aurelius Fulvus Boionius Arrius Antoninus)

Born 86   Reigned 138-161   Died 161

   He embarked early on a political career and was Consul in 120, received Tribunician powers each year after 138. He was adopted and made heir to the throne by Hadrian in 138, just prior to that emperor's death. Shortly after the death of Hadrian the Senate conferred on him the title "Pius". He had a peaceful and impartial reign. The Roman Empire enjoyed great prosperity under his rule and he was well liked. He adopted his nephew under a conditional agreement with Hadrian in order to gain his own adoption by that emperor. In 146 he celebrated the 900th anniversary of the founding of Rome with secular games. Unlike Hadrian, he never travelled far from Rome, instead he ruled the Empire from his palace in the capital.

"FAUSTINA, senior"
(*Annia Galeria Faustina*)

Born 105   Died 141

Faustina, senior, married Pius before he became emperor. She was the mother of Faustina, junior, later to become the wife of Marcus Aurelius. Her moral conduct was failing and she is reputed to have had many casual adulteries, all of which Pius attempted to conceal as he lavished every honor upon her. She died early in the reign of Pius in 141.

" MARCUS AURELIUS "
(*Marcus Aelius Aurelius Verus*)

Born 121   Reigned 161-180   Died 180

Marcus Aurelius, earlier called Marcus Annius Verus, was adopted by Antoninus Pius in 138 on the insistence of Hadrian who recognized great potential in the youth. He was declared Caesar and Consul in 138. Every year after 147 he was invested with the Tribunician powers. In 145 he married Faustina junior, the daughter of Pius. Upon the death of the emperor Pius he was declared emperor along with his step-brother Lucius Verus as his co-emperor in 161. This was the first of many uses of the device of shared rule in Rome's history. In this portrait he is shown in his late teens.

" MARCUS AURELIUS "

From the year 162 onward he campaigned strenuously in Germany and along the Danube to repel the destructive inroads of the united German tribes. At the same time Verus was dispatched to Syria, initiating the Parthian War, to subdue Parthian advances into the Roman protectorate of Armenia. Troops returning from the conclusion of the Parthian War in 166, brought with them a devastating plague. In this portrait Marcus Aurelius is shown at an age of about 45.

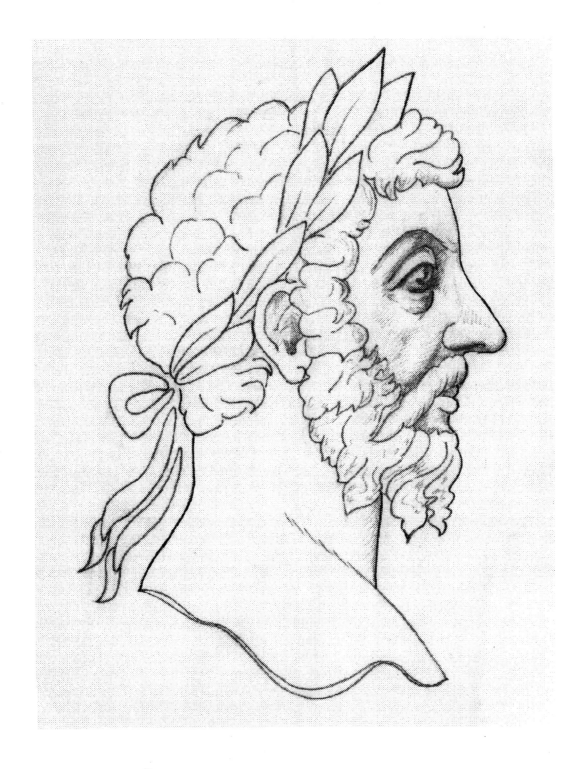

" MARCUS AURELIUS "

Except for a brief period, Marcus Aurelius was continually campaigning in the North. It was during the latter part of these campaigns that he wrote his famous "Meditations", a reflection on life by this stoic prince. The virtuous and philosophic conduct of his life and his gracious reign justly earned him the title "Philosopher King". This savior of the Roman Empire against the persistent and vigorous threats on its borders died in 180 at an age of 59. Here he is shown at an age of about 55.

" FAUSTINA, junior "
(*Annia Galeria Faustina*)

Born ca. 127   Died 175

Faustina junior was the daughter of Antoninus Pius and Faustina senior. She was married to Marcus Aurelius in 145, he was 24 at the time, she only 15. Faustina led a profligate life even more shameful than her mother. The emperor showed remarkable forbearance to her infidelities. She had several children, among others, Lucilla who married Lucius Verus, and a son the future emperor Commodus.

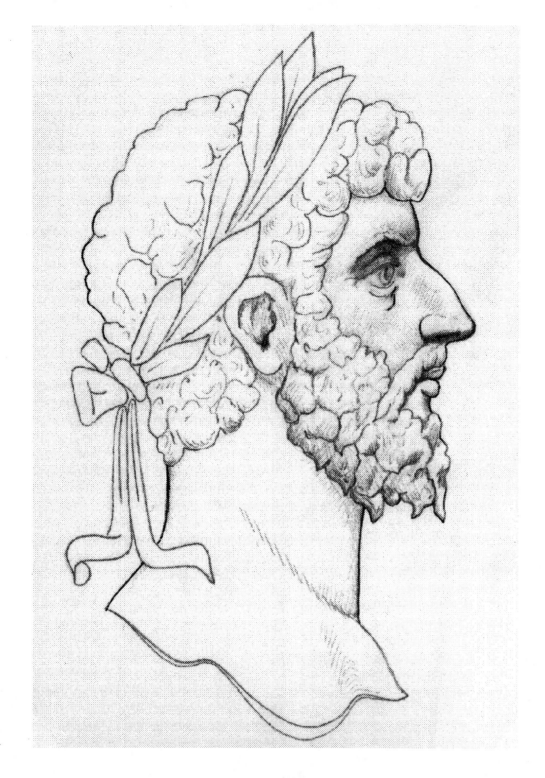

"LUCIUS VERUS"
(*Lucius Aurelius Verus*)

Born 130　　　　　　　　Reigned 161-169　　　　　　　　Died 169

He was the son of Aelius and adopted by Antoninus Pius in 138. Marcus Aurelius, his brother also by adoption raised him to joint sovereignty after the death of Pius. Verus and his generals fought a very successful campaign against the rebellious Parthians from 162 to 166. Verus was, however, an idle pleasure loving prince and distinctly the minor partner of Marcus Aurelius. Verus died of a stroke in 169.

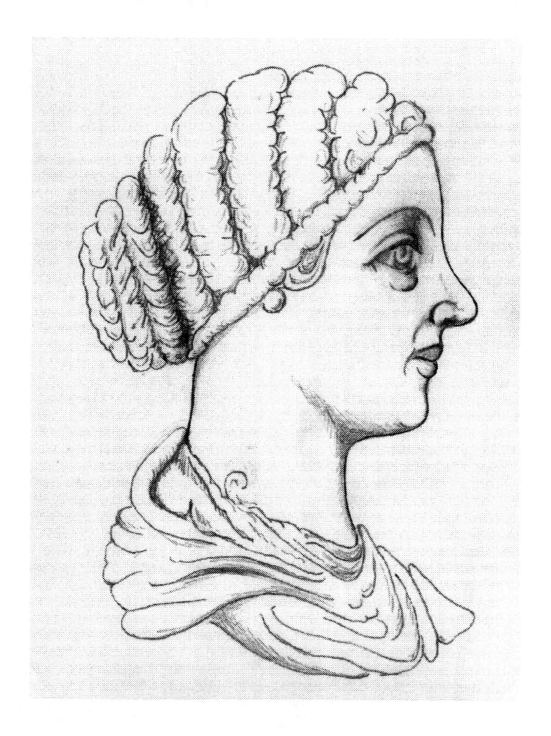

"LUCILLA"
(*Annia Aurelia Galeria Lucilla*)

Born ca. 147   Died ca. 183

Lucilla was the daughter of Marcus Aurelius and Faustina junior. She was married to Lucius Verus in 164. After his death she married C. Pompeianus, a Roman Senator. To her disgrace she later lived with her brother Commodus as his mistress. Abandoned by him, she unsuccessfully conspired against him. She was put to death while exiled to Capreae.

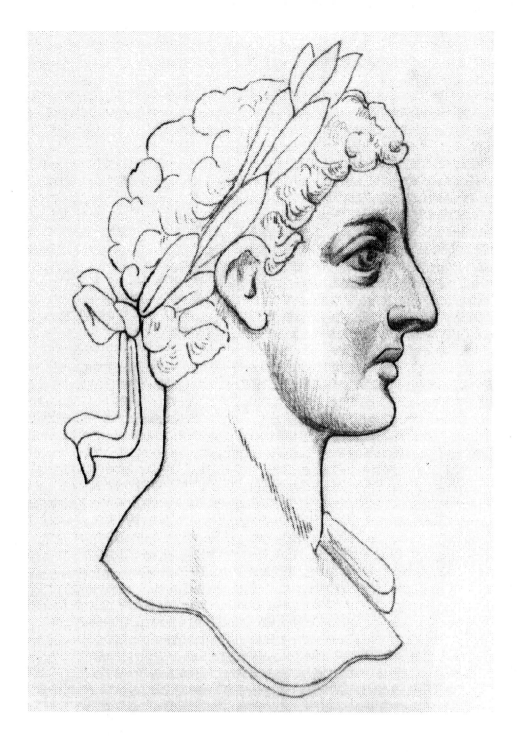

" COMMODUS "
(*Lucius Aelius Aurelius Commodus*)
Born 161   Reigned as Caesar 177-180, as Augustus 180-192   Died 192

Commodus was the son of Marcus Aurelius and Faustina junior. At age 5, in 166, his adoring father bestowed on him the title Caesar and elevated him to joint rule as Imperator Caesar in 177. From 178 onward he joined his father to fight on the Danube frontier. Upon the death of Marcus Aurelius in 180 he returned to Rome as emperor. He is shown in this portrait as a teenager.

" COMMODUS "

Commodus proved to be a great disappointment as emperor. He soon became a bloody megalomaniac abandoning ruling as emperor and descending to private depravities challenging the foul imperial reputations preceding the emperor Nerva. The actual running of the Empire was left to his chamberlains who in succeeding order were Perennis, Cleander, and Laetus, each replacing the murdered prior favorite. The present portrait is of him at an approximate age of 25.

" COMMODUS "

Commodus assumed the deified embodiment of Hercules upon himself and fought in gladiatorial contests and participated in the slaughter of animals in the amphitheater. After several failed plots against his life he was finally strangled while in a drunken (poisoned?) stupor in 192. This portrait depicts him at the age of about 30.

"CRISPINA"
(*Bruttia Crispina*)

Born ?   Died 183

A woman of great beauty she was married to Commodus in 177. Charged with adultery, she was divorced by Commodus and banished to Capreae, where she was strangled to death on his orders in 183.

"PERTINAX"
(*Publius Helvius Pertinax*)

Born 126   Reigned 193   Died 193

He was the son of a merchant and rose meritoriously through the military ranks to become Prefect of Rome in 189. The conspirators who plotted the murder of Commodus turned to Pertinax as the successor. Reluctantly Pertinax accepted the Purple in 193. Unfortunately he initiated a number of needed reforms too rapidly and incurred the displeasure of key constituencies including that of the army. A small force of praetorians stormed the palace and murdered Pertinax in 193 after a reign of only 87 days.

"DIDIUS JULIANUS"
(*Marcus Didius Salvius Julianus*)

Born 133 Reigned 193 Died 193

To the shame of Rome, the praetorian guard murderers of Pertinax held a public auction to select as emperor whoever offered them the greatest bribe. Didius Julianus, a wealthy Senator won the imperial prize by offering 25,000 sestertii per soldier. After a rule of only 66 days he was abandoned by the praetorians, who bowing to popular demand and the condemnation of the Senate murdered him.

" MANLIA SCANTILLA "
(*Manlia Scantilla*)

Born ?   Died ?

She was the wife of Didius Julianus, proclaimed "Augusta" by the Senate on the same day that her husband became emperor. Upon his death she was stripped of all her imperial titles and she died in obscurity.

"DIDIA CLARA"
(*Didia Clara*)

Born ca. 153   Died ?

She was the daughter of emperor Didius Julianus and Manlia Scantilla. At the accession of her father she was named "Augusta" by the Senate, but soon stripped of all titles after the death of her father. She was described as being a great beauty.

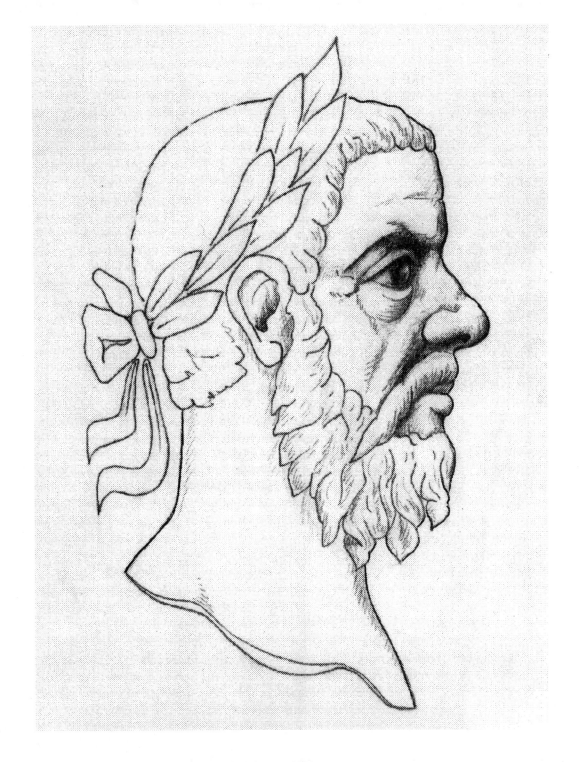

"PESCENNIUS NIGER"
(*Caius Pescennius Niger*)

Born ca. 135-140   Reigned 193-194   Died 195

Born to middle class parents he had a long and laudable career in the army and was appointed as commander of the army in Syria. Three rival emperors each proclaimed by their own soldiers appeared upon the death of Julianus; Niger in Syria, Albinus in Britain, and Severus in Pannonia. Niger lost his initiative by remaining in Antioch allowing Severus to secure Rome. Niger was defeated by Severus in 194 near Antioch, and fleeing he was overtaken and executed.

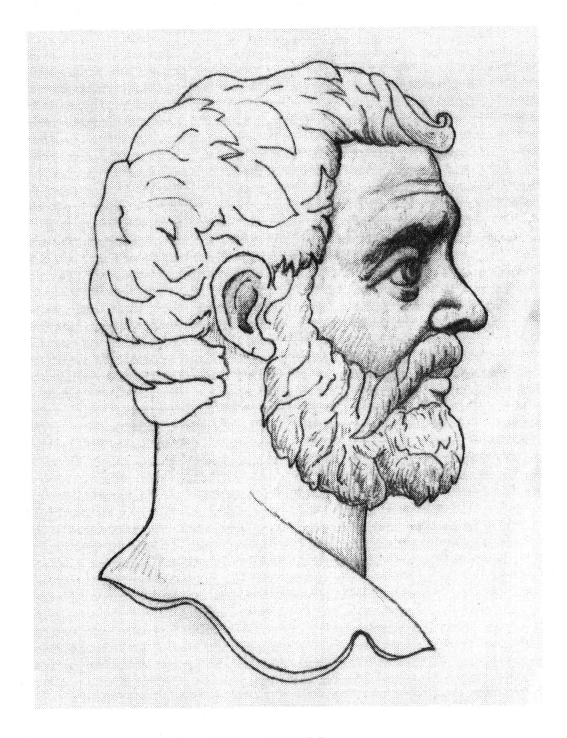

" CLODIUS ALBINUS "
(Decimus Clodius Septimius Albinus)

Born ?   Reigned as Caesar 193-195, as Augustus 195-197   Died 197

His skill and successes as a general gained him notice by Marcus Aurelius and Commodus and he was placed in command of the legions in Bithia. He was governor of Britain and Gaul at the time of Pertinax's death. To hold him in check while he dealt with Niger in the East, Severus offered Albinus the title of Caesar, which was accepted. However, as soon as Niger was dispatched, Severus attacked Albinus and in a decisive battle near Lyon in 197, he defeated Albinus who along with his wife and children were slain and their bodies thrown into the Rhone River.

"SEPTIMIUS SEVERUS"
(*Lucius Septimius Severus*)

Born 146   Reigned 193-211   Died 211

He was born in Lepcis Magna, a coastal city in modern Libya, which as emperor he lavishly adorned creating in the end a show piece city of Roman Africa. Severus was an able general and successfully carried out several civil appointments eventually leading to becoming governor of Upper Pannonia in 191. After the murder of Pertinax and the shameful ascendance of Julianus to the throne, the troops of Severus declared for him. He defeated rival candidates to the throne in military campaigns in rapid order; first Niger in 194, then Albinus in 197. He was awarded Tribuician powers in 193 and yearly thereafter. Severus was cunning and cruel in the extreme. He died in 211 while on an unfinished campaign to conquer Scotland.

"JULIA DOMNA"
(*Julia Domna*)

Born ca. 168   Died 217

  In 186 she was married to Septimius Severus as his second wife, being a young woman only about 18 years of age. The astrological horoscopes of the pair forecasted a successful marriage, a consideration important to the superstitious Severus. She had two sons by Severus, Caracalla in 188 and Geta in 189. She is shown in this portrait at about age 25.

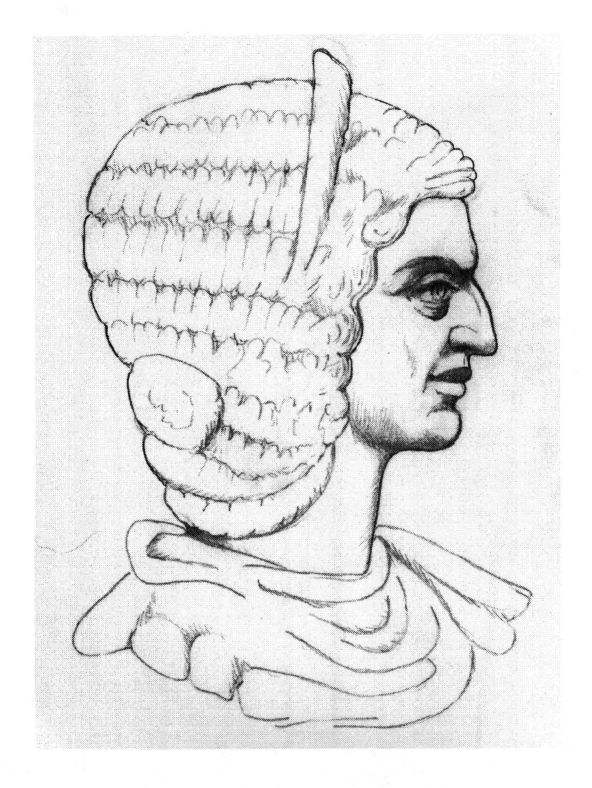

"JULIA DOMNA"

She was possessed of great intelligence and was a frequent advisor to Severus. After the death of Severus her life became bitter, particularly after she was forced to witness the murder of her youngest son Geta by Caracalla. Driven by despair, she committed suicide in 217. She is shown here at an approximate age of 45, the signs of discontent are clearly evident when a comparison is made with her earlier portrait.

"CARACALLA"
(*Marcus Aurelius Antoninus*)
Born 188 Reigned as Augustus 198-217 Died 217

Caracalla was the eldest son of Septimius Severus and Julia Domna. He was originally named Lucius Septimius Bassianus, the popular nick-name Caracalla is derived from a kind of Gaulish cloak he made fashionable in Rome. Severus conferred on him the title of Caesar in 196 and Augustus in 198. He ruled jointly with Severus and his brother Geta from 209 to 211, and upon the death of Severus with his brother for 10 months until 212. The two brothers hated each other since early boyhood and their joint rule ended with the murder of Geta by Caracalla. Caracalla was cruel and treacherous but loved by the army upon whom he showered many favors. He is noted for extending Roman citizenship on all freedmen in the Empire and for the construction of the famous Thermae Antoninae, the "Bath's of Caracalla". He was murdered by Macrinus while on a campaign in the East at an age of 29. He is shown here at a probable age of 25.

"PLAUTILLA"
(*Justa Fulvia Plautilla*)

Born ?   Died 212

She was the daughter of a very rich Praetorian Prefect Plautianus and married by her arrogant father to Caracalla in 202. The marriage was very bitter and hateful. Caracalla persuaded Severus to banish her to exile on the island Lipari upon the death of Plautianus in 205. After languishing in exile for seven years Caracalla, then emperor, had her murdered in 212 along with her daughter by him.

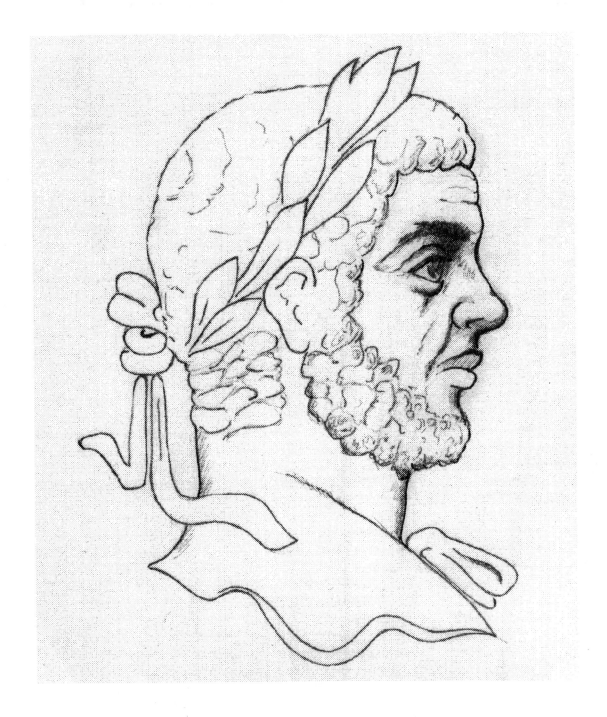

" GETA "
(*Lucius Septimius Geta*)

Born 189   Reigned jointly with Caracalla 209-212   Died 212

Geta was the youngest son of Septimius Severus and Julia Domna. Created Caesar by Severus in 198 and Augustus in 209, with the clear intention of the succession going to the joint rule of the brothers Geta and Caracalla. After the death of Severus, Caracalla ended the rivalry between the brothers by murdering Geta in 212 after a short joint rule. Caracalla sealed the deed by murdering many supporters of Geta. From age 20 onward Geta is shown on his coins with a short beard as depicted here.

"MACRINUS"
(*Marcus Opelius Severus Macrinus*)

Born 164   Reigned 217-218   Died 218

Macrinus was of Moorish descent, born in Caesarea, Mauretania, to a middle class family. He advanced in various appointments, finally to prefect of the praetorian guards under Caracalla. He was prime mover in disposing of Caracalla, if not in fact the actual murderer. Three days after the death of Caracalla he was proclaimed emperor by the troops and soon confirmed by the Senate. Upon his succession he did not return to Rome but continued the campaign against the Parthians initiated by Caracalla. This futile war was patched up by Macrinus in a settlement that paid the Parthians 200 million sestertii. Considered a disgrace by the army, they deserted him in open rebellion and defeated his loyal following at Antioch in 218. He tried to flee but was captured and executed.

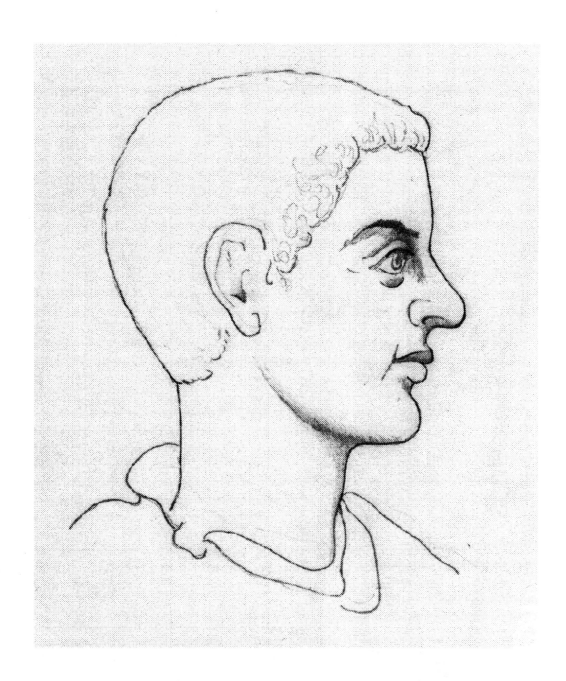

"DIADUMENIAN"
(*Marcus Opelius Antoninus Diadumenianus*)

Born 208   Caesar 217-218   Died 218

In an effort to conciliate a rebellious army, Macrinus appointed his son Diadumenian as Augustus in 218. This act was also partly to diffuse the rival claims on behalf of Elagabalus, then also a youth of age about 13. The effort failed and Macrinus attempted to save his son's life by sending him off to the Parthinians. He was overtaken and executed in 218. His portrait shown here is of him as a youth of age 9 or 10.

"ELAGABALUS"
(*Marcus Aurelius Antoninus*)

Born 205   Reigned 218 - 222   Died 222

   Originally named Varius Avitus Bassianus, the name by which he is popularly known refers to his appointment as a priest of the Sun-God Elagabalus during his boyhood. A rebellion started in the army around the district Emesa, probably instigated by his grandmother Julia Maesa, led to the defeat of Macrinus and the installation of Elagabalus as emperor in 218. He attempted to subordinate the position of all the Roman gods to that of the Sun-God Elagabalus. He was despised for his extreme debaucheries and cruelties. He and his mother Julia Soaemis were murdered while visiting the praetorian camp, their bodies beheaded, dragged through the streets of Rome, and finally thrown into the Tiber.

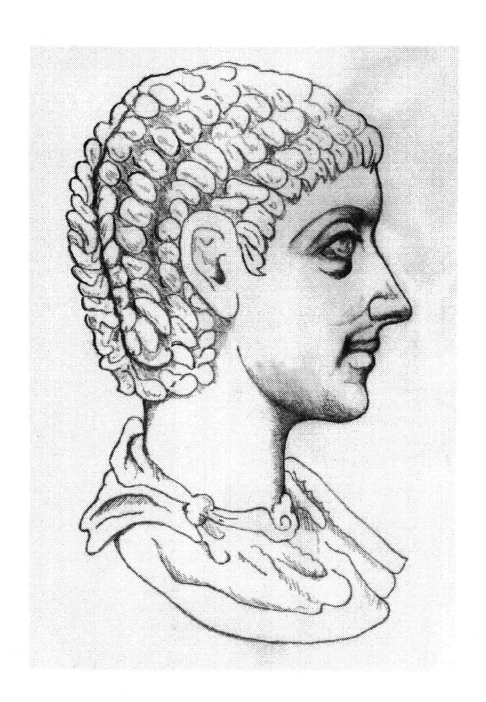

"JULIA PAULA"
(*Julia Cornelia Paula*)

Born ?   Died ?

She was the first wife of Elagabalus, married in 219 amid great pageantry and ceremony. Soon after nuptials she was divorced and stripped of her titles on some pretext of a bodily defect. She died in retirement.

" AQUILIA SEVERA "
(*Julia Aquilia Severa*)

Born ?   Died ?

She was the second wife of Elagabalus who married her in 220. She was taken from the sacred community of the Vestal Virgins by this dismal emperor to the great shock of Rome. Within a year she was deserted by Elagabalus who took Annia Faustina as his third wife, after he had her husband murdered. The emperor also deserted this new wife in less than a year and returned to Aquilia Severa.

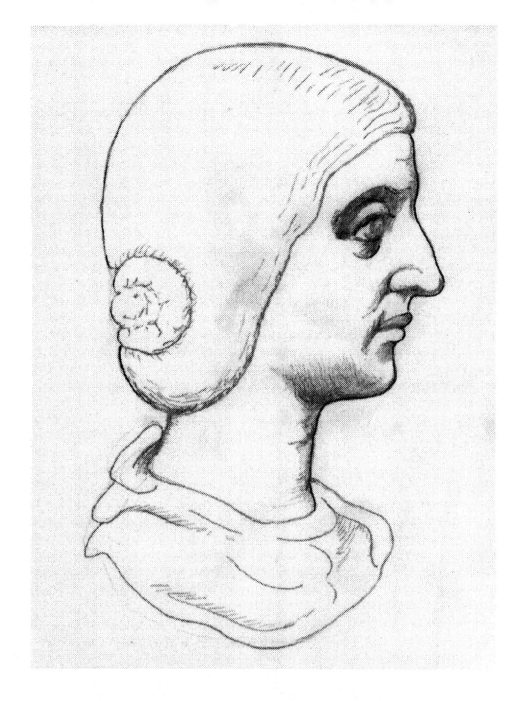

"JULIA SOAEMIAS"
(*Julia Soaemias*)

Born ?   Died 222

She was the daughter of Julia Maesa and the mother of Elagabalus who was born in 204. Widowed by the death of her husband Varius Marcellus she retired to Emesa after the death of Caracalla. She and her mother Julia Maesa engineered the insurrection against Macrinus and the elevation of Elagabalus to the throne. She was a devotee of the Sun-God cult of Elagabalus. She was a cruel woman and gave encouragement to the debaucheries of Elagabalus. She was put to death along with Elagabalus when they visited the praetorian camp in 222.

"JULIA MAESA"
(*Julia Maesa*)

Born ?   Died 224

   She was the daughter of Julius Bassianus, priest of the Sun-God, and the grandmother of Elagabalus. She was married to Julius Avitus, by whom she had Julia Soaemias, the mother of Elagabalus and Julia Mamaea, the mother of Severus Alexander. She possessed great wealth and her bribery of the soldiers stationed in the East to rise against Macrinus helped her and Julia Soaemias to place Elagabalus on the throne. She survived the murder of Elagabalus who she earlier had induced to adopt her grandson Severus Alexander as his heir. She died about the year 224 during the reign of Severus Alexander. Her portrait is shown at an advanced age, typical of her coinage.

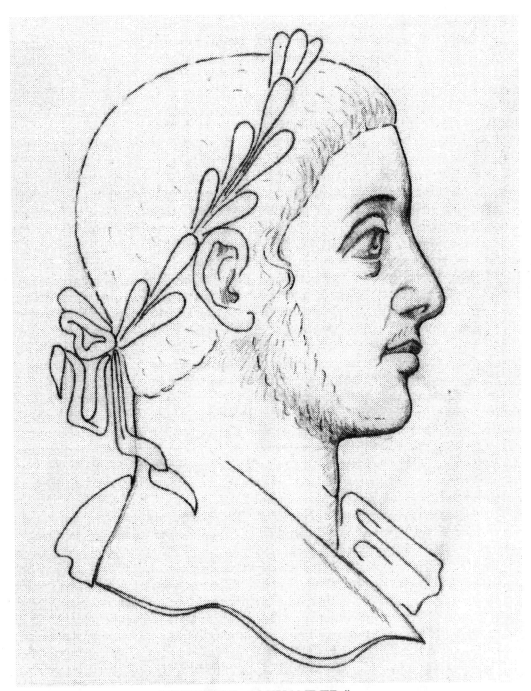

"SEVERUS ALEXANDER"
(*Marcus Aurelius Severus Alexander*)

Born ca. 208   Reigned 222-235   Died 235

   He was the son of Julia Mamaea, adopted by Elagabalus in 221 as Caesar and heir to the throne. His reign began upon the death of Elagabalus when only at an age of 14, with the joint regency established between Mamaea and her mother Julia Maesa. Upon the death of Maesa in 224, Mamaea became the sole advisor of Alexander, and wielded complete power in his name. She arranged for Alexander to marry Sallustia Orbiana in 225, as well as her banishment soon thereafter. War with the Parthians again erupted and Alexander was less than courageous as the commander, with the fighting resulting in a draw with great losses on both sides. Trouble also arose on the German border and while Alexander was preparing to repulse the German tribes, he was murdered along with Mamaea near Mainz in 235 by command of Maximinus, who was elevated by the emperor as one of the commanders of the army only to turn, in treason, against Alexander. Alexander is shown at an age of about 20 in the present portrait.

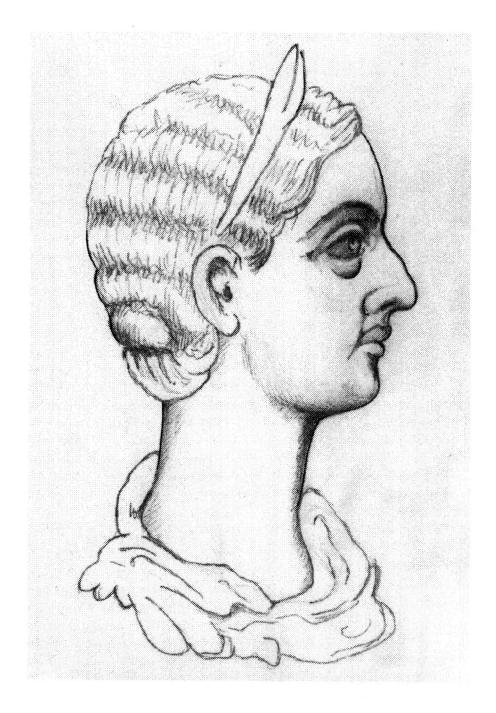

" ORBIANA "
(*Sallustia Barbia Orbiana*)

Born ?   Died ?

Julia Mamaea arranged for her son Severus Alexander to marry Sallustia Orbiana in 225. However, friction soon developed between the two women and in 227 Mamaea having grown jealous of Orbiana's status as Augusta had her exiled to North Africa. Alexander was so completely dominated by Mamaea that he did nothing to prevent this act.

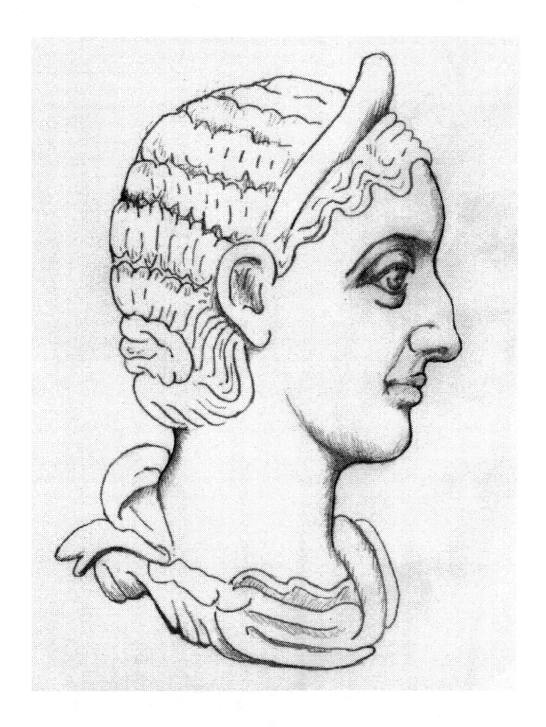

"JULIA MAMAEA"
(*Julia Mamaea*)

Born ? Died 235

She was the daughter of Julia Maesa and wife of Genesius Marcianus by whom she had Severus Alexander, born about 208. As guardian of Alexander she wielded enormous power, her domination of Alexander was such that he did exactly as he was told, she even selected his wife. Julia Mamaea accompanied Alexander on his campaign against the German tribes who had breached the Rhinland frontier. She was killed along with her son near Mainz, Germany, in 235 by their mutinous soldiers.

"MAXIMINUS I, THRAX"
(*Caius Julius Verus Maximinus*)

Born ca. 173   Reigned 235-238   Died 238

  Maximinus I, Thrax referring to his Thracian origin, was of peasant stock, a powerfully built man of great height. Uneducated, he adopted an army career enlisting as an ordinary soldier under the emperor Septimius Severus. He rose in rank and under Alexander he was made governor of Mesopotamia. He accompanied Alexander on the Rhinland campaign who gave him command of new army recruits. He turned on Alexander and had the emperor and his mother murdered in camp and was proclaimed emperor by the mutinous army. He concluded the German war with great success but was faced with numerous rebellions, most notable was the unsuccessful challenge by the Gordians in Africa in 238. That same year the Senate elected Balbinus and Pupienus as joint emperors. Maximinus invaded Italy (he had never set foot in Rome) but his troops mutinied and both he and his son Maximus were murdered in 238.

" PAULINA "
(Caecillia Paulina)

Born ?   Died ca. 235

Paulina was the wife of Maximinus I. She died sometime prior to the elevation of Maximinus to emperor, since all her coins show her vieled appropriate for commemorative issues.

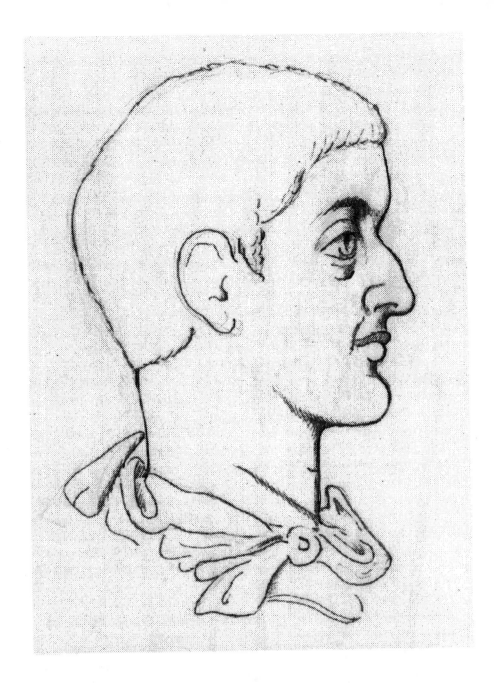

"MAXIMUS"
(*Caius Julius Verus Maximus*)

Born ca. 216 Reigned as Caesar 235-238 Died 238

Maximus was the son of Maximinus and presumably Paulina. After Maximinus was confirmed emperor by the Senate he raised Maximus to the title of Caesar. Although a handsome youth his arrogance led to general disliking of him. He joined his father in Germany and when they marched on Aquileia, Italy, to confront the jointly appointed emperors Balbinus and Pupienus, both father and son were murdered by their mutinous troops in 238. Maximus is shown here at an age of approximately 20.

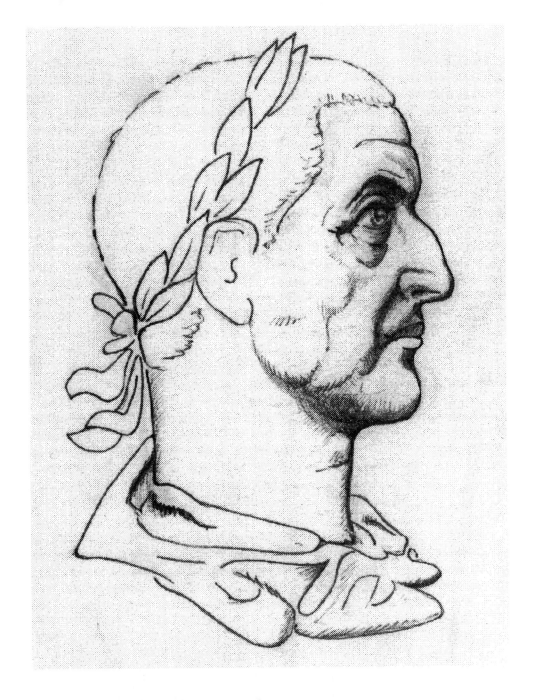

"GORDIAN I, AFRICANUS"
(*Marcus Antonius Gordianus*)

Born ca. 157   Reigned 238   Died 238

Gordian I (also called Gordian senior), was made Proconsul in Africa under Severus Alexander in 229, a position he also held during the reign of Maximinus I. He governed as an ideal Roman with moderation, virtue, and justice, as a result he was well regarded. He was a cultured man and excelled as a poet. In an uprising against Maximinus, Gordian was petitioned to become emperor. A delegation sent to Rome obtained confirmation by the Senate, who also declared Maximinus to be a public enemy. Before the delegation could return to Africa, Gordian (senior) had committed suicide when he heard of the death of his son (Gordian junior) in battle with the legion in Numidia that remained loyal to Maximinus.

"GORDIAN II, AFRICANUS"
(*Marcus Antonius Africanus*)

Born ca. 192　　　　　　　Reined 238　　　　　　　Died 238

Gordian II (also called Gordian junior), was the son of Gordian I. He was made his father's lieutenant by Severus Alexander in 229. When Gordian senior was declared emperor his son was also declared co-emperor. The only Roman legion in Africa was stationed in Numidia, it remained loyal to Maximinus and led by the provincial governor Capellianus easily defeated the local militia gathered by Gordian junior at Carthage. Gordian junior died in this battle in 238, after a joint rule with his father of only 20 days.

"BALBINUS"
(*Decimus Caelius Balbinus*)

Born ca. 178   Reigned 238   Died 238

The demise of the Gordian revolt left the rebellion supporting Roman Senate in jeopardy from the denounced Maximinus. To oppose Maximinus who was advancing on Rome, the Senate appointed as joint emperors the aging Balbinus and Pupienus. The populace was outraged at these selections of two patricians demanded and received the declaration of the 13 year old grandson of Gordian I as Caesar. The two emperors confronted Maximinus at Aquileia, in northern Italy. Maximinus and his son were murdered by their rebellious troops while besieging Aquileia.

" PUPIENUS "
(*Marcus Clodius Pupienus Maximus*)

Born ca. 164   Reigned 238   Died 238

Pupienus was appointed joint emperor with Balbinus by the Senate primarily to oppose Maximinus. When Maximinus was murdered by his own troops the two emperors fell into dispute concerning the division of power between them. This ill-timed confrontation led the praetorians, who were never pleased with the Senatorial appointment of the emperors, to revolt and brutally murder the two aged men after their rule of only 99 days.

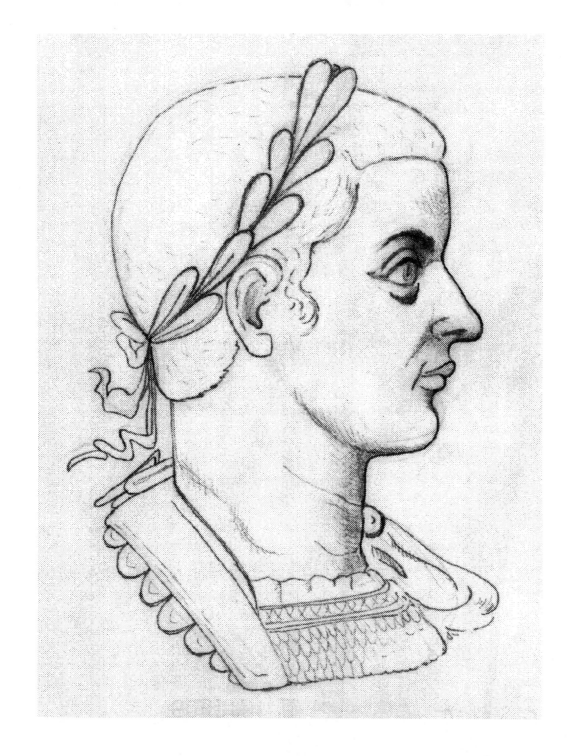

"GORDIAN III"
(*Marcus Antonius Gordianus*)

Born 225   Reigned 238-244   Died 244

Gordian III was the son of Maecia Faustina, the daughter of Gordian I. The joint emperors Balbinus and Pupienus raised Gordian to the rank of Caesar and after the murder of the co-emperors the praetorian guard proclaimed him emperor in 238 at age 13. Embarked on an expedition against the Persians, he was murdered by his own troops who were incited by Philip I to depose the young emperor in 244 at age 19.

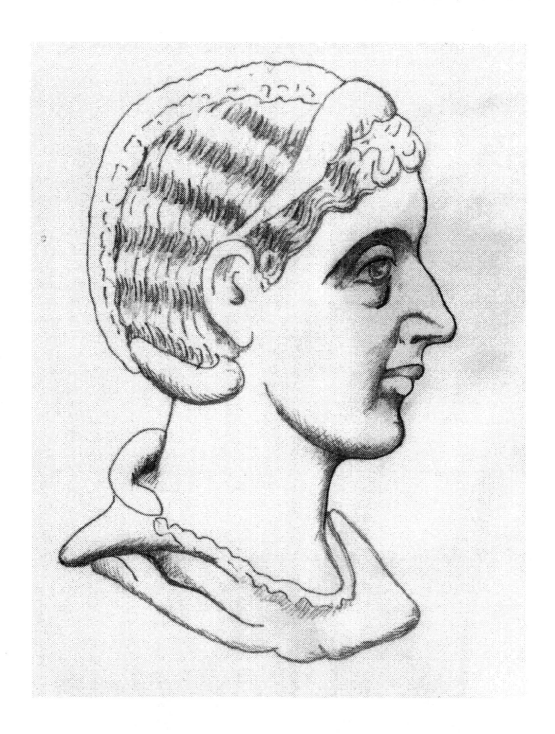

" TRANQUILLINA "
(*Furia Sabina Tranquillina*)

Born ?   Died ?

She was the daughter of Timisitheus the praetorian prefect and Prime Minister of Gordian III. Tranquillina was married to Gordian III in 241. She was a person of great moral virtue and merit. She survived the murder of her husband but her subsequent fate in life is unknown.

"PHILIP I, the ARAB"
(*Marcus Julius Philippus*)

Born 204 Reigned 244-249 Died 249

Philip I was a native of Arabia who rose through the military ranks to the post of praetorian commander appointed by Gordian III. While this young emperor was in the field during the Persian campaign, Philip through treachery undermined the loyalty of the troops, had him murdered and himself proclaimed emperor. Philip was, none the less, a conscientious ruler. Philip mounted a spectacular celebration in 248, for the 1000th anniversary of the foundation of Rome. He was defeated and killed in a war against Decius in 249.

"OTACILIA SEVERA"
(*Marcia Otacilia Severa*)

Born ?   Died ?

She was the wife of Philip I married to him about 234, prior to his elevation to the imperial throne. While ambitious, she led a private life without reproach. Under her protection the Christians worshipped in peace, she may have professed to Christianity and subjected herself to serving penance for her complicity in the death of Gordian III. Upon the death of Philip and her son she died in retirement.

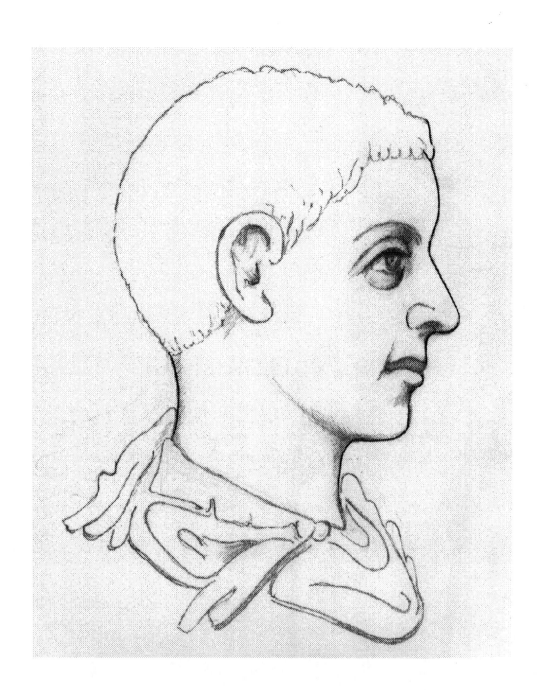

"PHILIP II"
(*Marcus Julius Philippus*)

Born ca. 238 Reigned 247-249 Died 249

He was proclaimed Caesar in 244 on the accession of his father Philip I to the throne, at a young age of about 6. His father elevated him to the rank of Augustus in 247. He was killed by the praetorian guard when word arrived in Rome that Philip I had been murdered.

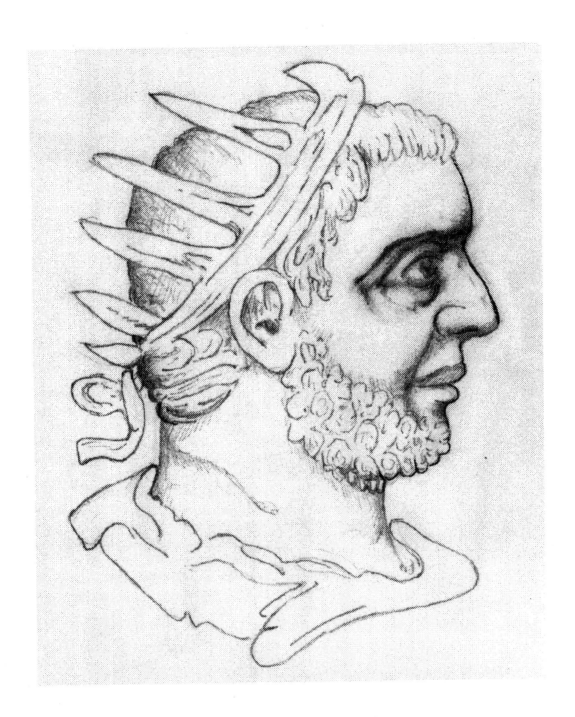

"PACATIAN"
(*Tiberius Claudius Marinus Pacatianus*)

Born ca. 218   Reigned ca. 248   Died ca. 248

Pacatian was a usurper who seized power for a brief period in Moesia or Pannonia, eventually murdered by his own troops. What very little that is known about him is all based on the analysis of his coin issues. One reverse suggests that he sought some kind of accommodation with Philip I. His coins show him about an age of 30.

"JOTAPIAN"
(*M. Fulvius Rufus Iotapianus*)

Born ? Reigned ca. 248 Died ca. 248

The harsh rule and financial burden imposed on the eastern provinces by Priscus, the brother of Philip I, who was given overall charge for these provinces led to an uprising in Syria with the troops declaring for Jotapian. Jotapian was soon murdered by his own troops after a short reign. Not much further is known about this emperor.

"TRAJAN DECIUS"
(Caius Messius Quintus Traianus Decius)

Born ca. 198   Reigned 249-251   Died 251

He was born in lower Pannonia to a family of rank. He was an energetic soldier and a distinguished senator and made the governor of Moesia and lower Germany. He was dispatched by Philip I to suppress the rebellious troops and the usurpers it spawned in the eastern provinces. However, these troops perhaps fearing severe retribution, immediately demanded a very reluctant Decius to accept the title of Imperator, threatening his death if he refused. Thus installed he proceeded south towards Rome with his troops and engaged Philip's forces in a battle near Verona. Philip was defeated and slain. The Senate conferred the Purple on Decius in 249. As emperor he displayed many admirable traits, but to his discredit he exercised great repression of the Christians. In 250 Decius embarked on a major campaign against a strong invasion by the Goths. His army fell into a trap while pursuing the enemy in Thrace and was badly defeated. Decius and his son Etruscus were killed in 251 after a reign of less than two years. In this portrait he is shown at an age of about 50, the burden of heavy responsibility weighing on his shoulders is evident in his lined visage.

"HERENNIA ETRUSCILLA"
(*Herennia Etruscilla*)

Born ?   Died ?

Decended from an Italian family of rank, she was the wife of Trajan Decius and had two sons by him, Herennius Etruscus and Hostilian. Not much else is known about this empress.

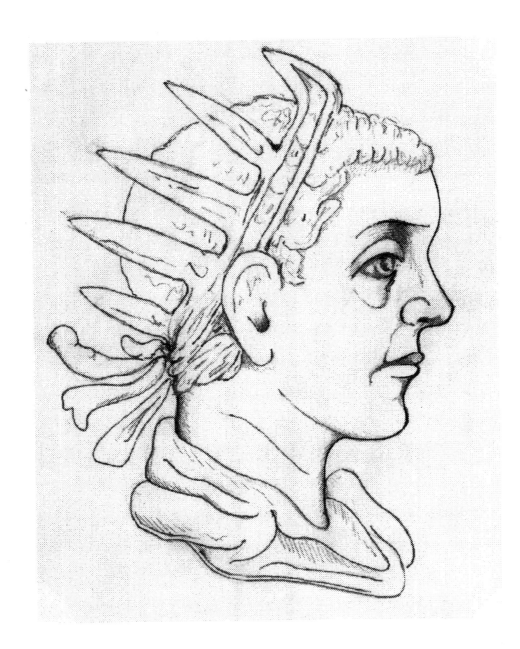

" HOSTILIAN "
(*Gaius Valens Hostilianus Messius Quintus*)

Born ?   Reigned 251   Died ca. 251

  Hostilian was the younger son of Decius and given the rank of Caesar by his father in 251, at the same time that his elder brother Herennius Etruscus was named Augustus. Upon the death of his father and brother on the field of battle, Trebonianus Gallus the new emperor raised Hostilian to the rank of Augustus, which was also confirmed by the Senate. He died shortly thereafter of the plague.

" TREBONIANUS GALLUS "
(*Caius Vibius Trebonianus Gallus*)

Born ca. 206　　　　　　Reigned 251-253　　　　　　Died 253

   Gallus had a leading role in Decius' war against the Goths and was possibly implicated in the defeat and death of Decius in the trap set by the Goths in 251. Upon the death of Decius and his eldest son Herennius Etruscus the army declared for Gallus who also appointed Hostilian, the remaining son of Decius, as co-emperor. Gallus quickly concluded a dishonorable peace with the Goths and returned to Rome, devastated by a raging plague that also took the life of Hostilian. The Goths broke the agreement with Gallus and again invaded the north eastern provinces. The governor of upper Moesia, Aemilian, dealt a severe defeat to the Goths and was immediately declared emperor by his troops and marched on Rome. Gallus raced north to engage Aemilian and in a battle near Terni Gallus was defeated and he and his son Volusian were slain in 253.

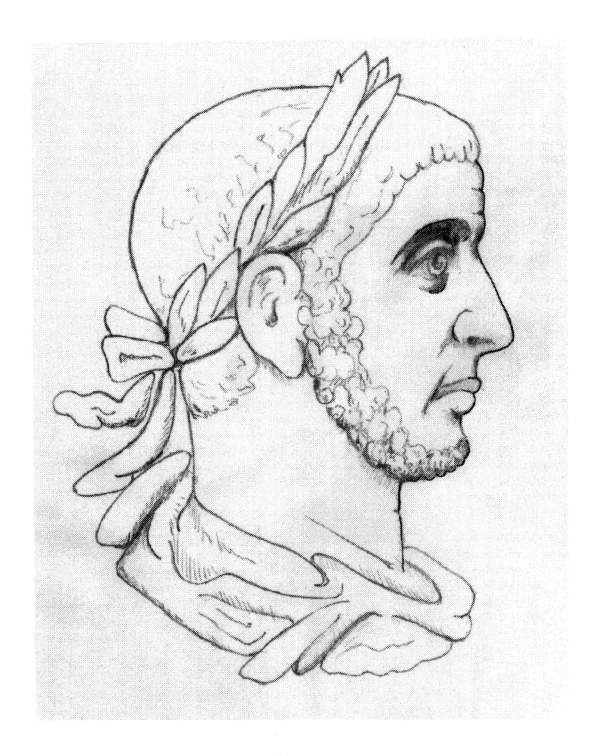

"VOLUSIAN"
(*Caius Vibius Volusianus Trebonianus*)
Born ?   Reigned 251-253   Died 253

Volusian was the son of Trebonianus Gallus. His father bestowed the rank of Caesar on him at the time of his accession to the throne in 251. When the co-emperor Hostilian died soon thereafter, Volusian was declared Augustus and co-emperor with Gallus. Volusian was slain along with his father in a battle with Aemilian in 253.

"AEMILIAN"
(*Marcus Aemilius Aemilianus*)

Born 207   Reigned 253   Died 253

He was a good soldier, received highest dignities and was appointed governor of Moesia and Pannonia. He repulsed an invasion by the Goths with great slaughter. Upon this victory he was hailed as Augustus by his troops and he marched on Italy. He defeated the opposing army of Trebonianus Gallus and Volusian, the two co-emperors having been killed by their own troops prior to battle. He then took the field against the challenger Valerian I who was also proclaimed emperor. Aemilian in turn was also murdered by his own troops prior to any military action, he ruled for only 88 days.

"URANIUS ANTONINUS"
(*L. Julius Aurelius Sulpicius Uranius Antoninus*)
Born ? Reigned ca. 253-254 Died ca. 254

He was a priest-king of the capital city of Emesa who successfully defeated the Persian army attacking the city in 253. As a result he declared himself as a claimant to the throne and was eliminated as a rival by Valarian in 254. Not much is known about this ruler.

"VALERIAN I"
(*Caius Publius Licinius Valerianus*)

Born ca. 195   Reigned 253-260   Died ?

Valerian was a major military commander under Gallus and summoned to help him in confronting Aemilian. His forces arrived too late to extricate Gallus from defeat. Upon the death of Gallus and the murder of Aemilian by his own troops, Valerian was declared emperor by the army and acknowledged by the Senate in association with his son Gallienus as co-emperors. Valerian initiated a vigorous campaign against the Persians in 254, who were ravaging the Syrian provinces. After some successes he foolishly agreed to a personal meeting with the Persian king Sapor and was captured alive in 260. Accounts vary, but Valerian appears to have spent the remainder of his life as a captive in abject misery and degradation..

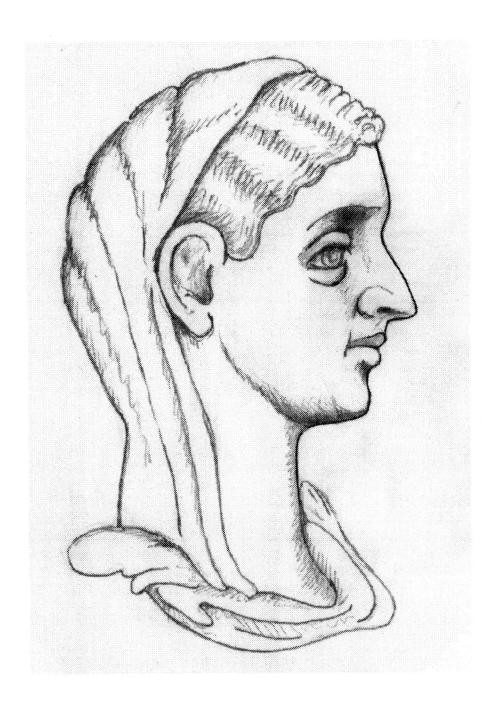

"MARINIANA"
(Egnatia Mariniana)

Born ?   Died ?

She was the wife of Valerian I and likely predeceased him prior to his accession to the imperial purple. The coins of Mariniana were all issued posthumously.

"GALLIENUS"
(*Publius Licinius Egnatius Gallienus*)

Born ca. 215   Reigned 253-268   Died 265

Gallienus was the son of Valerian I and was elevated with his father to the rank of co-emperors in 253. He had principal responsibility for governing the Western Empire while Valerian's concern was the Eastern. Upon the capture of Valerian by Sapor, Gallienus became the sole emperor in 260. In spite of being beset by civil wars, foreign invasion and the plague, he had time for poetry and the pursuing of the arts. Much of the Roman East was lost and in 259 Gaul, Spain, and Britain were lost to Postumus. Gallienus was murdered by his own soldiers in 268 while in the midst of conducting the Gothic Wars and repulsing the usurper Aureolus.

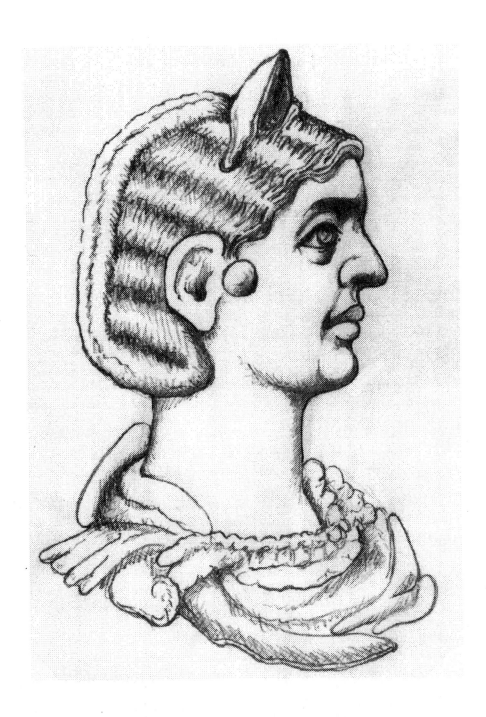

" SALONINA "
(*Julia Cornelia Salonina*)

Born ?   Died 268

Salonina married Gallienus about the year 244 and was named Augusta when her husband became joint emperor with Valerian in 253. She was beautiful and exhibited great wisdom and virtue without ostentation. She perished with Gallienus when they were murdered in Milan in 268.

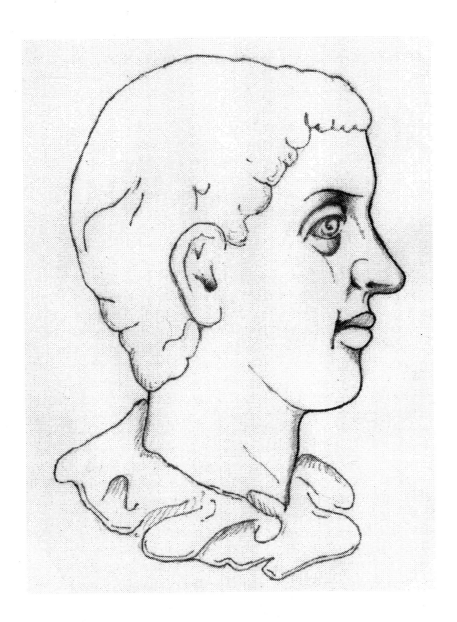

" SALONINUS "
(*P. Licinius Cornelius Saloninus Valerianus*)

Born ? Reigned 259 Died 260

Saloninus was the younger son of Gallienus and Salonina. He was left in control of Colonia Agrippina (Cologne) by Gallienus who was engaged in campaigns against the German tribes along the Danube and Rhine accompanied by his eldest son Valerian II. He was declared Augustus when his brother died in 258, possibly of natural causes. Saloninus and his guardian Silvanus were surrendered to Postumus who had besieged Cologne in 260. They were promptly executed.

"MACRIANUS"
(*Fulvius Junius Macrianus*)

Born ? Reigned 260-261 Died 261

After the capture of Valerian by the Persians in 260, they continued to overrun the Eastern provinces but were checked by Valerian's general Ballista aided by the Macriani, the father and his eldest son. Buoyed by this success the two Macriani set out for Italy to challenge Gallienus in 261 but were met in the Balkans and defeated and killed by Gallienus' general Aureolus. The younger son Quietus was left at Emesa in charge of Syria. He was captured and killed by the king of Palmyra in 261. This portrait is based on a superb aureus with the legend : IMP.C.FVL. MACRIANUS P.F. AVG and is undoubtedly for the eldest son Macrianus junior or sometimes referred to as Macrianus II. No Latin inscribed coins of the father Macrianus I are known. Virtually all coins of Macrianus II and his brother Quietus show indistinguishable crude portraits.

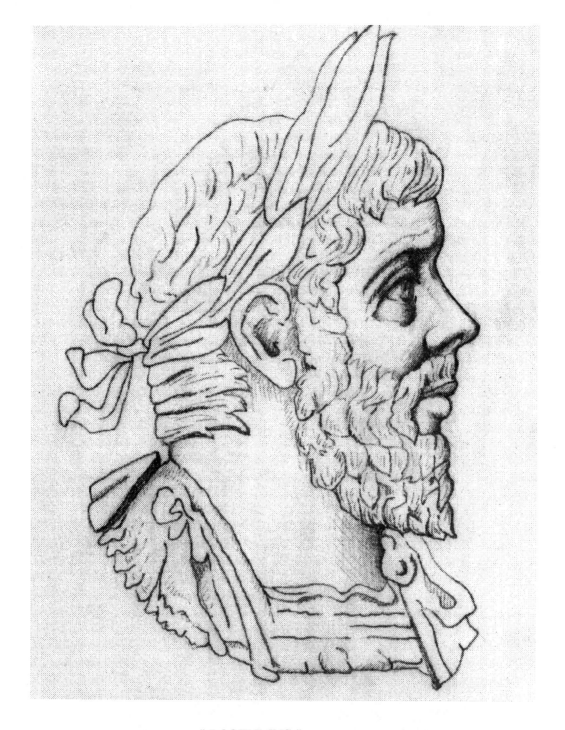

" POSTUMUS "
(*Marcus Cassianus Latinus Postumus*)

Born ? Reigned 259-268 Died 268

Postumus was an able soldier of humble origins who was awarded the command of the Rhine legions in Gaul by the emperor Valerian. Soon after the capture of Valerian the loyalty of Postumus to Gallienus ended with the troops proclaiming him emperor in Gaul, Spain, and Britain, 260-261. Gallienus advanced against Postumus in 265 only to withdraw when wounded in battle. Thereafter Postumus successfully ruled his Gallic empire and established a secure Rhine frontier. He was murdered by his troops when he forbad the sacking of the captured city of Mainz won in a battle against the usurper Laelianus in 268.

" LAELIANUS "
(*Ulpius Cornelius Laelianus*)

Born ? Reigned 268 Died 268

He was governor of upper Germany under Postumus and led a rebellion in Mainz against this Gallic emperor in 268. His revolt was quickly defeated and Mainz retaken. Surprisingly his defeat resulted in the murder of Postumus by the angered troops when they were denied the pillaging of the captured city. Not much else is known about this usurper.

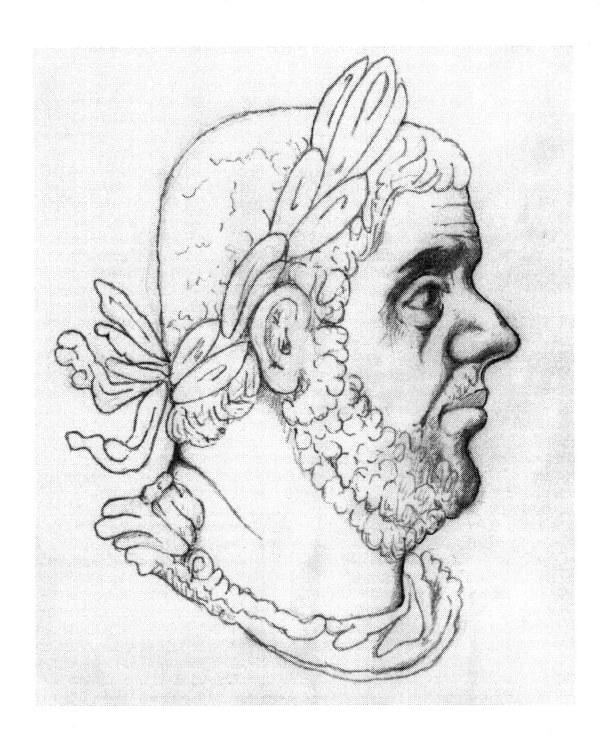

"MARIUS"
(*Marcus Aurelius Marius*)
Born ?   Reigned 268   Died 268

He was a blacksmith and armorer by trade. He rose from the military ranks to the status of a general. On the death of Postumus he was declared emperor by his Gaulish legions. After a very short reign of at most two or three months he was murdered by his army comrades in 268 using, it is said, a sword that he himself fabricated.

" VICTORINUS "
(*Marcus Piavvonius Victorinus*)

Born ?   Reigned 265-271   Died 271

He was an able military figure and was chosen by Postumus as a colleague in 265. During the turmoil following the death of Postumus, Marius seized power for a very brief period and upon his death Victorinus became the sole Gallic emperor in 268. Weakened by the seceding of the Spanish provinces and attacked by the Roman emperor Claudius II, the Gallic empire was rapidly disintegrating. Victorinus did succeed in suppressing a revolt in central Gaul at Autun only to be murdered by his own entourage shortly afterwards at Cologne in 271.

"TETRICUS I"
(*Caius Pius Esuvius Tetricus*)

Born ?　　　　　　　　　Reigned 270-274　　　　　　　　　Died ?

Upon the death of Victorinus his wealthy mother Victoria bought the allegiance of the legions in order to elevate Tetricus senior to the Gallic throne in 271. He was a popular choice and an excellent military commander. In 273 he bestowed the title of Caesar on his son. The Roman emperor Aurelian marched against father and son in 274 and in a fierce battle near the Gallic capital of Trier the two Tetrici were defeated. They both surrendered to Aurelian and were pardoned and continued in senior administrative positions in other parts of the Empire. Thus ended the Gallic empire after a 15 year of independence of Rome.

"CLAUDIUS II, GOTHICUS"
(Marcus Aurelius Claudius)

Born 214   Reigned 268-270   Died 270

He was born in Illyricum and held important military commands under Valerian and Gallienus. After Gallienus was killed in Milan, Claudius in a reserve command nearby was declared emperor in 268 and quickly concluded operations against the usurper Aureolus. He crushed an immense army of Goths in 269 for which victory he received the title Gothicus Maximus. He was well loved by the Senate and the people and was a model emperor. While continuing the campaign against the Goths he succumbed to the plague in 270, much mourned. The imperial power passed to his brother Quintillius who reigned for about one month when the Danube legions under his command declared for Aurelian and he committed suicide.

" QUINTILLUS "
(*Marcus Aurelius Claudius Quintillus*)
Born ?   Reigned 270   Died ca. 270

The younger brother of Claudius Gothicus, Quintillus was declared emperor by his troops at Aquileia upon the death of Claudius. Aurelian, also declared emperor marched against Quintillus who finding himself abandoned by the very troops that elected him emperor, committed suicide by having his veins opened. He reigned very briefly, never having left Aquileia during this entire period of his short rule.

"AURELIAN"
(Lucius Domitius Aurelianus)

Born 214　　　　　　　　Reigned 270-275　　　　　　　　Died 275

He was born of an obscure family in Pannonia and had a distinguished military career rising to the post of general of the cavalry under Claudius Gothicus. After the death of Claudius and the suicide of Quintillus he assumed the purple in 270. He fought a successful campaign against Germanic invasions and in the East defeated and captured the secessionist Palmyrene Queen Zenobia. He restored Roman control over the Gallic empire when Tetricus I surrendered to him. Both Queen Zenobia and Tetricus were displayed as captives in a spectacular triumphal celebration in Rome in 274 and Aurelian was declared " Restitutor Orbis " for reuniting the Roman empire to its former extent. He was engaged in numerous construction projects to adorn the city and initiated the first defensive fortified wall around Rome. He was murdered in a conspiracy in 275.

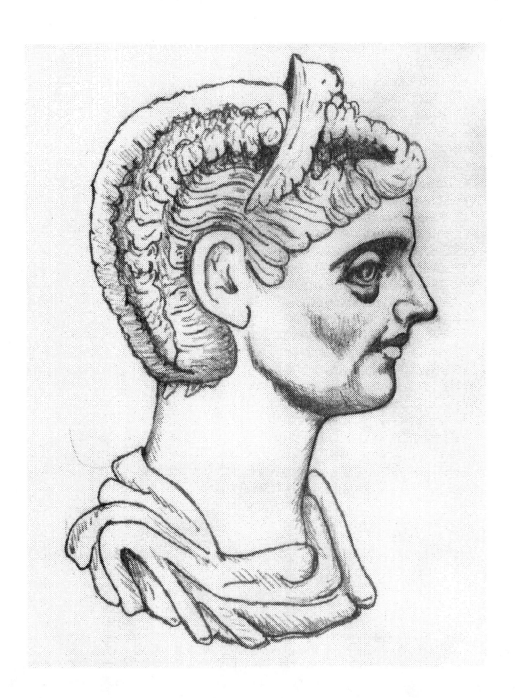

"SEVERINA"
(*Ulpia Severina*)

Born ?   Died ?

Severina is thought to have been the daughter of Ulpius Crinitus, a renowned general in Valerian's time who adopted Aurelian and presumably gave him his daughter in marriage. She apparently survived her husband.

"TACITUS"
(*Marcus Claudius Tacitus*)

Born ca. 200　　　　　Reigned 275-276　　　　　Died 276

For a six to eight month period after the death of Aurelian there was no one as the head of state until the Senate supported by the army selected M.C. Tacitus as emperor. He was a man of integrity, honor, and cultured in the pursuit of literature. He joined the army in Thrace, picking up where Aurelius left off in the defense of the Eastern provinces, and delivered a decisive defeat on the invading Goths. Somewhere in Thrace on his return to Rome in 276 he died either of a fever or an assassination.

"FLORIANUS"
(*Marcus Annius Florianus*)
Born ?   Reigned 276   Died 276

He was the half-brother of Tacitus who he joined in the struggle against the Goths in the East. When Tacitus died he was acknowledged emperor by the Senate and all the provinces except Syria where the army declared for Probus. Tacitus immediately marched against Probus, but ciil war between the two factions was averted when Florianus was killed by his own troops at Tarsus, after a rule of only two or three months.

"PROBUS"
(Marcus Aurelius Probus)

Born 232   Reigned 276-282   Died 282

Probus was born in Pannonia of obscure parents, an able commander who rose in stature under the emperors Valerian, Claudius, and Aurelian and was made governor of the Eastern provinces under Tacitus. After the death of Florianus his accession to the throne declared by the army was confirmed by the Senate in 276. He was victorious in defeating all the numerous assaults on the Empire from all corners of the frontier. He was a just and able ruler who completed the defensive wall around Rome begun by Aurelian. He devoted great attention to the restoration of economic life of the Empire, particularly in Gaul which had been devastated by the marauding invasions of the barbarians for too many years. He however, earned the discontent of the army in forcing them to participate in many non-military assignments which may have led to his murder by mutinous troops near Sirmium in 282.

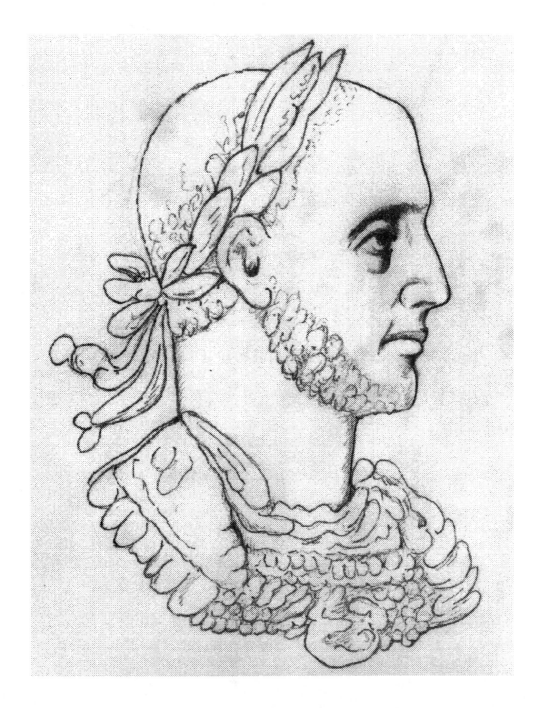

" CARUS "
(*Marcus Aurelius Carus*)

Born ca. 224   Reigned 282-283   Died 283

  After holding various civil and military offices he was made prefect of the Praetorian guard by Probus. Upon the death of Probus he was declared emperor by the legion in Pannonia and confirmed by the Senate. Carus named both his sons, Numerian and Carinus, Caesar. Carus and his younger son Numerian secured the Danube frontier and set off on a campaign against the Persians. Carinus was left with governing of the Western empire. Carus triumphed against the Persians, capturing their capital at Ctesiphon on the Tigris River. However, Carus died while encamped at Ctesiphon, killed by lightning or more than likely assassinated by his own troops.

"NUMERIAN"
(*Marcus Aurelius Numerianus*)

Born ca. 253 Reigned 283-284 Died 284

He was the younger son of Carus and accompanied him on the Persian campaign in 283 when his rank was elevated from Caesar to Augustus. Following the death of Carus he broke off the Eastern campaign and slowly proceeded back towards Rome. He lost his sight to an eye infection and had to be carried in a litter offering a tempting target and was murdered by his praetorian commander Arrius Aper. Aper was seized, tried by a military tribunal, and put to death by Diocletian, commander of the body guard.

"CARINUS"
(*Marcus Aurelius Carinus*)

Born ca. 250   Reigned 283-285   Died 285

He was the oldest son of Carus and was left in charge of the Western provinces while Carus and his younger son Numerian campaigned in the East. Carinus was declared Augustus by his father in 283. With the death of both Carus and Numerian, Carinus became sole emperor. Carinus successfully campaigned in Britain in 284. The next year he marched against Diocletian who was advancing from the east. During a battle between the two rivals in 285 near modern Belgrade, he was murdered by his own army who then also declared for Diocletian. Perhaps fueled by propaganda on behalf of Diocletian the rule of Carinus is described as that of a cruel, vindictive, and sexually depraved monster.

"MAGNIA URBICA"
(*Magnia Urbica*)

Born ?   Died ca. 285

  The emperor Carinus of bisexual appetite, accumulated numerous "wives" but only Magnia Urbica appears to have been officially proclaimed his wife. She died about the same time as Carinus in 285.

"JULIAN, of PANNONIA"
(*Marcus Aurelius Julianus*)

Born ? Reigned 284-285 Died 285

He was a rebellious general in Pannonia under Carinus, proclaimed emperor in that region in 284. Carinus marched against Julian and he was defeated and slain near Verona, Italy in 285.

"DIOCLETIAN"
(Caius Aurelius Valerius Diocletianus)

Born 245 Reigned 285 - 305 Died 313

A competent general and statesman, he held important commands under the emperors, Probus, Aurelius, and Carus. He was proclaimed emperor after the assassination of Carinus in 285. Instability along the long borders of the empire required the appointment of a co-Augustus, Maximianus I (Herculius) in 286. The governance and defense of the vast empire soon demanded additional imperial colleagues. Constantius I (Chlorus) and Galerius were installed as Caesars in 293. The Empire was divided into four separate domains, each with one of the four imperial colleagues as immediate ruler. This organization constituted the First Tetrarchy. In 305 both Diocletian and Maximianus abdicated as planned and were replaced by Galerius and Costantius as Augusti. Two new Caesars, Severus II and Maximinus II (Daza) were appointed. Quarrels and internal rivalries brought this admirably crafted organization of orderly succession to an end before Diocletian's death in retirement in the year 313.

"CARAUSIUS"
(*Marcus Aurelius Mausalus Carausius*)

Born 245 ?　　　　　　　Reigned 287 - 293　　　　　　　Died 293

   Appointed commander of the fleet stationed at Boulogne by emperor Maximianus Hercules, he was instructed to end the predatory expeditions of the Franks and Saxons against the Atlantic coastal settlements. He turned virtual pirate himself. Maximianus ordered his death, but he escaped from his stronghold at Boulogne to Britain. There he was proclaimed emperor in 287. He was assassinated by his chief minister Allectus in 293.

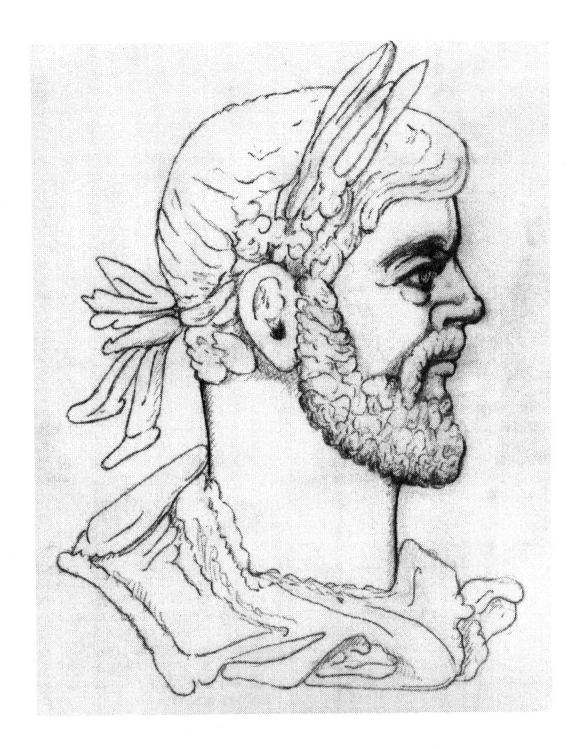

"ALLECTUS"
(*Caius Allectus*)

Born ?   Reigned 293-297   Died 297

Allectus, the chief minister of Carausius, assassinated this Britainic emperor in 293 and had himself proclaimed emperor. Constantius Chlorus while in Gaul prepared an invasion fleet which in 297 landed in Britain and defeated and slew Allectus, thus returning Britain to the Roman Empire after a ten year separation.

"DOMITIUS DOMITIANUS"
(*Lucius Domitius Domitianus*)

Born ? Reigned 296-297 Died 297

He was an obscure usurper who declared himself emperor in Alexandria while in command of the Egyptian legions under the reign of Diocletian. He was murdered after a short reign of a year or so, only to be replaced by another usurper in Alexandria, Aurelius Achilleus who was met and defeated by Diocletian in 298.

" MAXIMIANUS I, HERCULES "
(Marcus Aurelius Valerius Maximianus)

Born ca. 250   Reigned 286-305, 306-308, 310   Died 310

Maximianus I, Hercules was born in Pannonia of humble origin and served with distinction under Aurelian and Probus. He was designated Augustus and co-emperor by Diocletian in 286. Resigned the purple in 305 at the same time Diocletian voluntarily abdicated as per the plan of the tetrarchy structure. The previously named Caesars in 293, Galerius and Constantius, automatically became the new Augusti in 305. Two new Caesars, Severius II and Maximianus II, Daza were appointed. The untimely death of Constantius in 306, spawned a fierce competition among the protagonists for power. The revolt of Maxentius in Rome who declared himself Augustus in 306, brought his father Hercules Maxentius back as co-emperor for his support. This second reign for Maximianus lasted from 306-308. Caught in a further intrigue in 310 he was ordered to commit suicide.

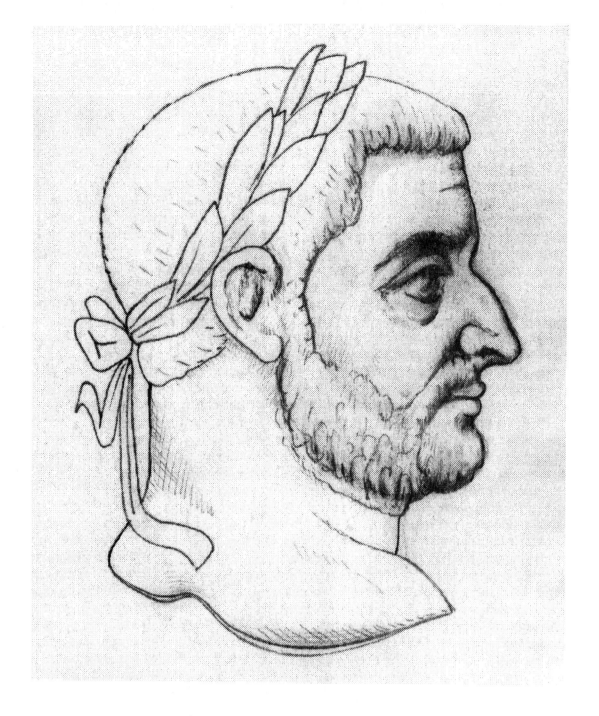

" CONSTANTIUS I, CHLORUS "
(*Flavius Valerius Constantius*)
Born ca. 250   Reigned as Caesar 293-305, as Augustus 305-306   Died 306

In the governmental design of the Tetrachy created by Diocletian, Constantius I was designated Caesar in 293 and on the abdication of Diocletian he was elevated to rule as Augustus. In successful campaigns, he defeated Allectus and restored Britain to Roman rule in 297, and in 305 he defeated the Picts in Caledonia. He was generally of poor health, hence the nickname " Chlorus (the pale) ". He succumbed to disease in 306 in York. He was the father of Constantine the Great, by his wife Helena.

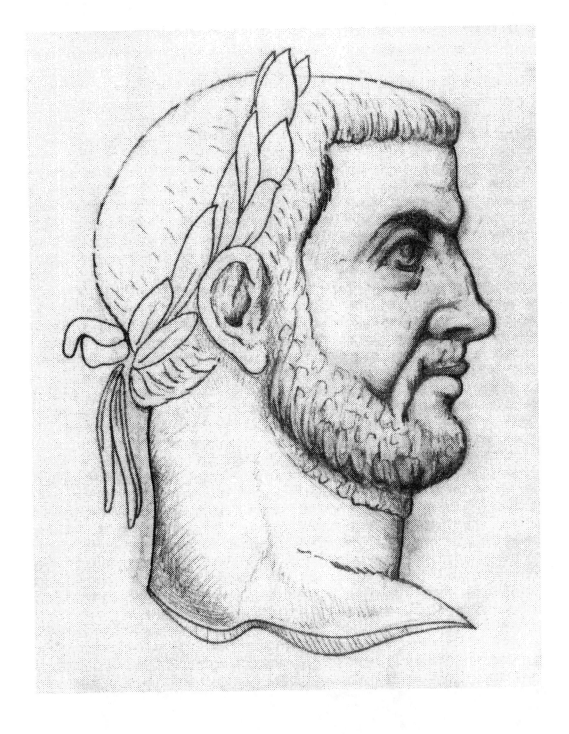

"GALERIUS"
(Caius Galerius Valerius Maximianus)

Born ca. 260　　Reigned as Caesar 293-305 as Augustus 305-311　　Died 311

Under the planned rules of succession of the Tetrarchy, he was named Caesar in 293 and Augustus in 305. After suffering a heavy defeat at the hands of the Persians in 297 he regrouped and with a decisive victory eliminated the Persian threat in the East for some time. At the strong urging of Galerius a pitiless persecution of the Christians occurred during the late Tetrarchy. He died of a horrible illness in 311. At his death bed he renounced his anti-Christian edicts.

"GALERIA VALERIA"
(*Galeria Valeria*)

Born ?   Died 307

She was the daughter of Diocletian and married Galerius in 293 as his second wife. On the death of Galerius, Maximinus Daza offered to marry her, which at her peril she rejected and was banished to Syria. After Daza's death she escaped to the court of Licinius only to be mistreated and eventually beheaded.

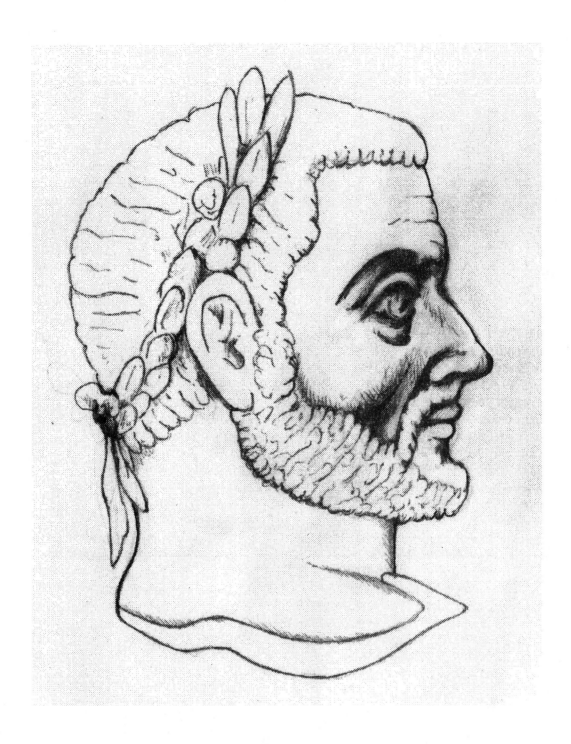

" SEVERUS II "
(*Flavius Valerius Severus*)
Born ?   Reigned as Caesar 305-306, as Augustus 306-307   Died 307

He was appointed Caesar in 305, and raised to Augustus in 306 by Galerius to become the senior emperor in the West. Maxentius proclaimed himself emperor in 306 and was immediately confronted by Severus. Prior to a battle at the outskirts of Rome, Severus was deserted by his own army, forced to abdicate and to commit suicide.

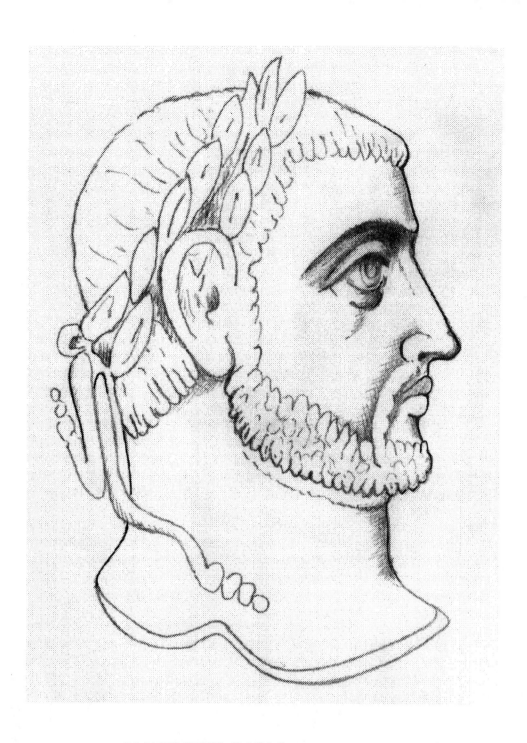

"MAXIMINUS, DAZA"
(*Galerius Valerius Maximinus*)

Born 270   Reigned as Caesar 303-308, as Augustus 309-313   Died 313

He was named Caesar in 305 and governed in the Eastern provinces. He proclaimed himself Augustus in 308, and in 313 allied himself with Maxentius against Constantine and Licinius. In a decisive battle in Thrace Licinius defeated Daza, who fled to Tarsus, where to avoid capture he poisoned himself. His wife and children were put to death. During his reign he revealed himself a brutal and cruel tyrant, and a persecutor of the Christians.

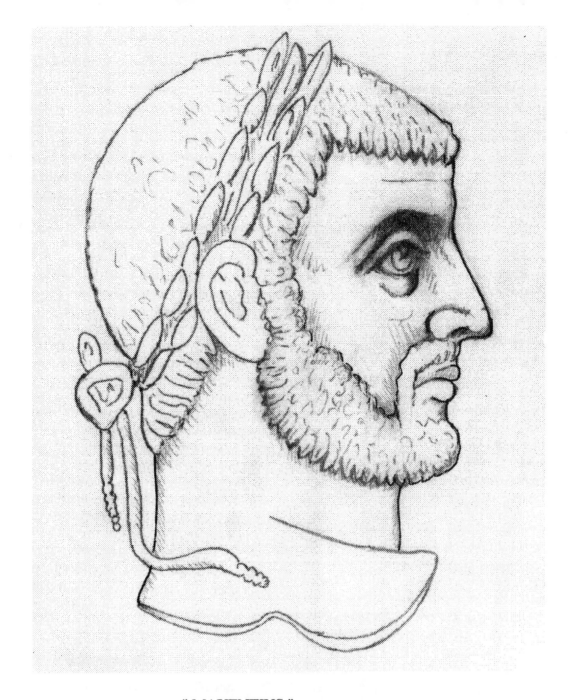

"MAXENTIUS"
(*Marcus Aurelius Valerius Maxentius*)
Born 282   Reigned as Caesar 306, as Augustus 306-312   Died 312

   He was the son of Maximinus Hercules. Being passed over when the first Caesars were appointed to the Tetrarchy and once again when Severus and Maximinus Daza were proclaimed the next set of Caesars, his smoldering indignation led to a revolt in Rome whereupon he was proclaimed Caesar and rapidly thereafter emperor in 306. This was also the year Chlorus died in Britain and was replaced by his son Constantine (the Great) who was proclaimed emperor. Galerius and Severus both failed at deposing Maxentius, Severus being killed in the effort. In 312 Constantine defeated the much larger army of Maxentius at the famous battle of the Milvian Bridge to the west of Rome and Maxentius drowned while attempting to escape. The six year reign of Maxentius earned him a reputation as a cruel and sanguinary tyrant.

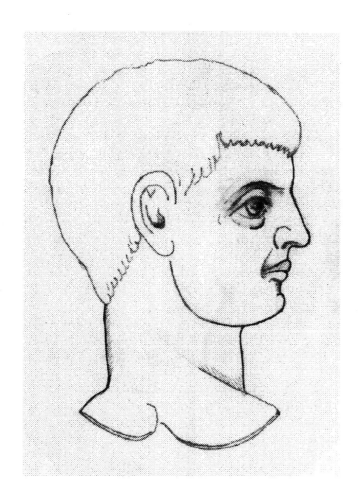

" ROMULUS "
(*Marcus Aurelius Romulus*)

Born ca. 305   Died ca. 309

He was the son of Maxentius who declared him both Caesar and Augustus while Romulus was still very young. However, he died at an early age of about four, thus dashing his father's hope of establishing a dynasty. All his coins were issued posthumously.

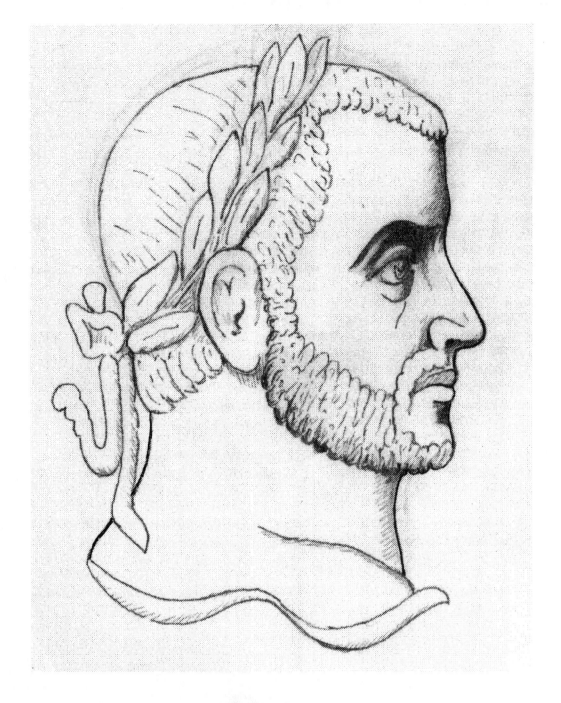

"LICINIUS, I"
(*Publius Flavius Claudius Galerius Valerius Licinianus*)

Born 265   Reigned 307-324   Died 324

He was born of an obscure Dacian family, fought successfully against the Persians and was named Caesar and Augustus as an outcome of the famous Congress at Carnuntum in 308. Licinius and Constantine (the Great) were allied against Maximinus Daza and Maxentius. Daza was dispatched 313 by Licinius and Maxentius in 312 by Constantine, leaving Licinius and Constantine sharing the rule of the Empire, Constantine in the Western provinces and Italy, and with Licinius controlling the Balkans and the East. The uneasy alliance was shattered in 316 but led to a military stalemate, until in 324 when Constantine moved in strength against Licinius who was defeated, surrendered, and soon killed.

" CONSTANTINE, the GREAT "
(Flavius Valerius Aurelius Constantinus)

Born ca. 273   Reigned as Caesar 306-308, as Augustus 308-337   Died 337

He was the son of Constantius Chlorus and Helena. He joined his father in Britain in 297 to campaign against Allectus. When Chlorus died in 306, Constantine was proclaimed Augustus by the legions in Britain. At the time in 308 when Galerius called the imperial conference at Carnuntum there were six claimants to the imperial throne. In the final conference conclusions, Constantine was demoted to Caesar and Maximianus Hercules was forced to renounce his imperial titles. When Galerius died in 311, Constantine and Licinius formed an alliance against Daza and Maxentius. Constantine, in the famous battle at the Milvian Bridge in 312 defeated Maxentius, Constantine openly adopted Christianity for himself and his legions displayed the sign of the cross on their imperial standards and shields. The two emperors Daza and Maxentius were eliminated by 313, however, the victors, Constantine and Licinius, envious of each other, soon quarreled and in 324 Constantine defeated Licinius and ordered his strangulation. He moved his capital in 330 to Byzantium and renamed it Constantinople. Although Constantine adopted the Christian faith as early as 312 and pagan sacrifices and gladiatorial contests were forbidden by 324, it was the issuance of the Nicene Creed in 325 and his baptism on his death bed in 337 that truly conferred the title of the "First Christian Emperor" on him.

"HELENA"
(*Flavia Julia Helena*)

Born 248   Died 328

She was the first wife of Constantius Chlorus, whom she married prior to his elevation to the rank of Caesar in 295. She was the mother of Constantine the Great. Helena travelled in the Holy Land to discover the sites of the events in the Gospels, most notably she reputedly found the tomb of Christ in Jerusalem, whereupon Constantine then built the Church of the Holy Sepulcher.

"FAUSTA"
(*Flavia Maxima Fausta*)

Born ?   Died 326

She was the daughter of Maximianus Hercules, sister of Maxentius and second wife of Constantine the Great, whom she married in 307. She gave birth to Constans, Constantine II, and Constantius II. She was suffocated in a boiling hot bath by order of Constantine in 326 for having caused the death of Crispus she falsely accused and when the truth became known.

"CRISPUS"
(Flavius Julius Crispus)

Born ca. 300   Reigned as Caesar 317- 326   Died 326

Crispus was the son of Constatine the Great by his first wife Minervina. He was made Caesar in 317 along with his half-brother Constantine II and Licinius II. Crispus was a prince of noble virtues and talents and of considerable military skill. His help was crucial in defeating the Franks in 320 and destroying the fleet of Licinius I at Gallipoli in 323. After the defeat of Licinius I in 324, the father and son Licinii were executed and Constantine named another half-brother of Crispus, Constantius II as Caesar. In 326, Fausta the mother-in-law of Crispus, jealous that the popular Crispus would eclipse her three sons (Constans was her son born in 320), she fabricated false evidence against Crispus, which Constantine believed and had Crispus executed. Fausta paid the ultimate penalty when the truth was discovered, and Constantine repented in great sorrow.

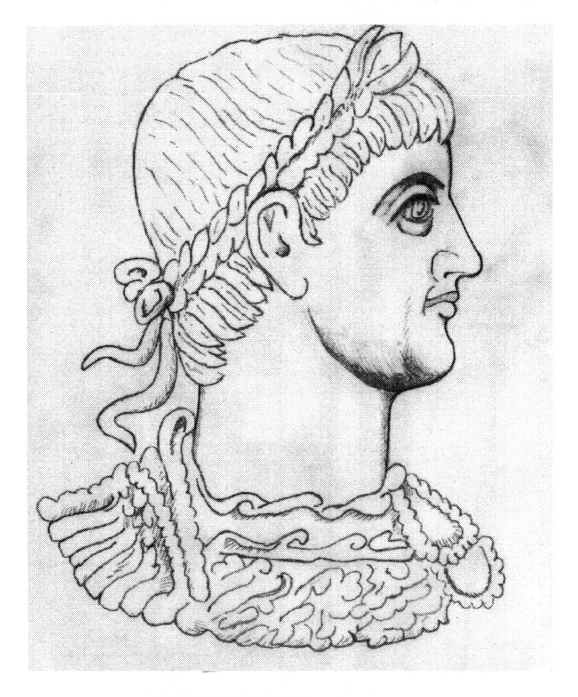

"CONSTANTINE II"
(*Flavius Claudius Julius Constantinus*)
Born 314   Reigned as Caesar 317-337, as Augustus 337-340   Died 340

He was the first son of Constantine the Great by his second wife Fausta and was created Caesar in 317. In 332 while only 18 years old, he successfully campaigned against the Goths with much slaughter. In 333 Constantine divided the rule of the Empire amongst his three sons, Constantine II, Constans, and Constantius II, and his two nephews, Delmatius and Hanniballianus. Upon the death of Constantine the Great, and the murder of Delmatius and Hanniballianus, a new alignment of imperial order commenced with the three sons declared Augusti. Constantine II received Spain, Gaul, and Britain as his provinces. Unsatisfied with his share he made territorial demands against Constans, who refused. In 340 Constantius II invaded Italy, the province of Constans, only to have his army ambushed and cut to pieces, he himself dying in the battle.

"CONSTANS"
(*Flavius Julius Constans*)

Born ca. 320   Reigned as Caesar 333, as Augustus 337-350   Died 350

He was the youngest of the three sons of Constantine the Great by his second wife Fausta. He was created Caesar in 333, at an age of about 13. In the division of the Empire in 337 after the death of Constantine, he received as his provinces to rule, Italy, Illyria, and Africa. Upon the defeat of Constantine II, who treacherously invaded Italy when his territorial demands against Constans was refused, Constans found himself the undisputed emperor of the West. In 343 he established calm in Britain becoming the last ruling emperor to visit that island. In 350, while in Gaul he received word of a revolt in the army with Magnentius proclaimed emperor, fled, but was overtaken near the Pyrenees and murdered.

"CONSTANTIUS II"
(Flavius Julius Constantius)

Born 317   Reigned as Caesar 324-337, as Augustus 337-361   Died 361

He was the second son of Constantine the Great by his wife Fausta. He was declared Caesar in 324 at the tender age of 7. In the division of the Empire after the death of Constantine in 337 and the arrangements made soon there after, he acquired as his share the entire East including Thrace and Egypt. Most of his rule was spent combating Persian incursions. In 350, however, receiving word of the death of Constans and the elevation of Magnentius to emperor of the West, he proceeded to march against this usurper. After several losses in the field Magnentius committed suicide in 353, leaving Constantius II sole emperor of the entire Roman Empire. He elevated his half-cousin Julian as Caesar and junior colleague in 355. Julian's popularity aroused Constantius to march against him in 360, but before any military encounter Constantius died of a fever in 361.

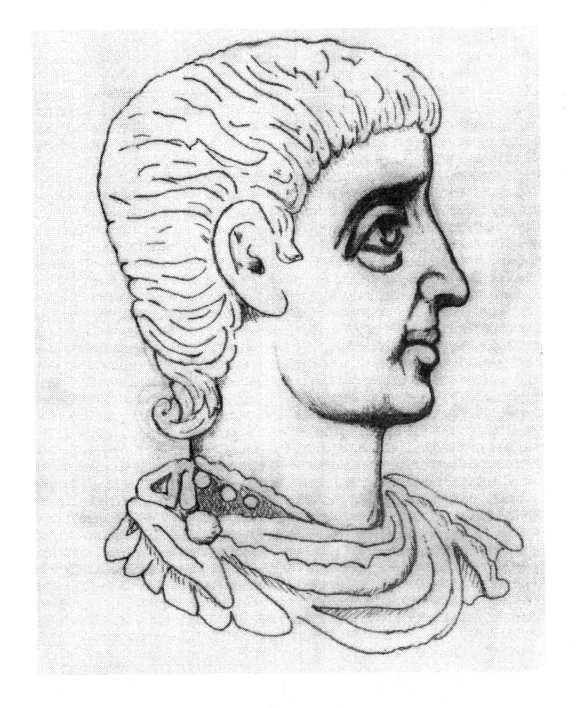

"HANNIBALLIANUS"
(*Flavius Claudius Hanniballianus*)

Born ? Reigned as Rex 335-337 Died 337

He was the nephew of Constantine the Great and the brother of Delmatius. Constantine appointed him governor of the province Cappadocia and Armenia with the title Rex (king) in 335, as part of his wish for the division of the Empire between his three sons, Constantine II, Constans, and Constantius II, and his nephews the brothers Delmatius and Hanniballianus. At the same time Delmatius was elevated to the rank of Caesar and awarded rule over Thrace, Macedonia, and Achaia. However, after the death of Constantine the army decided that only his sons should rule and the brothers were executed in 337.

"MAGNENTIUS"
(Flavius Magnus Magnentius)

Born 303   Reigned 350 - 353   Died 353

He was a soldier of great ability and the favorite of his mentor Constans, in 350 he ungratefully repaid the kindnesses Constans showed him by instigating a rebellion that deposed the emperor and thereby allowed him to usurp the rule of the Western provinces. He recklessly attacked Constantius II in an attempt to become the master the entire Roman Empire. His total military defeat led to his fleeing to Lyon where, abandoned by his army, he committed suicide in the year 353.

" DECENTIUS "
(*Magnus Decentius*)

Born ?   Reigned as Caesar 351-353   Died 353

Decentius was the brother of Magnentius, who in 351 elevated him to the rank of Caesar and sent him to defend Gaul beyond the Alps, where he gained very little success. On his way to come to the assistance of Magnentius he received word of that usurper's death and rather than be captured he committed suicide in Sens in 353.

"NEPOTIAN"
(*Flavius Popilius Nepotianus Constantius*)

Born ? Reigned 350 Died 350

He was a nephew of Constantine the Great. He was Consul in 336 and in the turmoil following the death of Constans in 350, he declared himself emperor by seizing power in Rome. He unjudiciously turned the inhabitants of Rome against himself through proscriptions and murderous cruelties. After a short rule of 28 days, he was killed in a battle with Marcellianus, a general of Magnentius.

" VETRANIO "
(*Vetranio*)

Born ?   Reigned 350-351   Died 357

The legions under Vetranio's command in Illyria and Pannonia proclaimed him emperor following the death of Constans in 350. Constantius II marched against him in 351 and prior to battle near Serdica, Vetranio abdicated in the presence of Constantius. Constantius treated him with kindness and allowed him to live out the rest of his life in retirement in Bithynia where he died in about the year 357.

"CONSTANTIUS GALLUS"
(Flavius Claudius Constantius)

Born 325   Reigned as Caesar 351-354   Died 354

Gallus was the son of Constantius Chlorus, nephew of Constantius II and half-brother of Julian II. He was created Caesar in 351, and assigned the defence of the Eastern provinces against the Persians and sent to reside in Antioch. Inspite of his affiliation to the Christian Church he inspired the dread and hatred of his subjects by his cruel and unjust behavior. The emperor Constantius II apprised of his atrocious conduct lured Gallus to a supposed meeting in Milan, had him arrested on the way, tried, convicted, and beheaded.

" JULIAN II, the APOSTATE "
(*Flavius Claudius Julianus*)

Born ca. 332   Reigned as Caesar 355-360, as Augustus 361-363   Died 363

   Julian was the half-brother of Gallus and nephew of Constantine the Great. He was created Caesar in 355 by Constantius II and made governor of Gaul, Spain, and Britain. Julian was a man of learning and scholarship as well as a great general, with many triumphs against the invading barbarians. In religious matters he preferred paganism to Christianity and gained in approbation the title of "Apostate". In 360 the troops in open revolt against Constantius declared him emperor. Constantius on his way to confront Julian died of fever in 361, leaving Julian sole emperor. Julian while campaigning against the Persians was wounded and died in 363.

"JOVIAN"
(*Flavius Claudius Jovianus*)

Born 331   Reigned 363-364   Died 364

Jovian was a military commander under Julian II and when that emperor died in 363 while campaigning against the Persians, Jovian was declared the new emperor by the army. He made a less than honorable peace with the Persians in order to extricate the Roman army from Persia. He restored privileges to the Christians revoked by Julian and supported the Nicene Creed. After reigning for little more than four months he died of suffocation when a charcoal brazier was accidentally left in his tent while encamped in Bithynia on his way to Constantinople.

"VALENTINIAN I"
(*Flavius Valentinianus*)

Born 321   Reigned 364-375   Died 375

He was of humble origin but achieved high military rank under both Julian and Jovian. Upon the death of Jovian he was elected emperor by the army and civil officials in 364. He appointed his younger brother Valens as a joint Augustus assigning him the Eastern provinces, while keeping the rule of the Western provinces for himself. In 367 Valentinian appointed his eldest son Gratian, then only 8 years old, as Augustus. Valentinian spent most of his reign repulsing barbarian incursions along the Rhine and Illyricum. In 375 during a conference with the Quadi invaders of Illyricum that he in great fury at their insolence had a stroke and expired.

" VALENS "
(*Flavius Valens*)

Born 328 Reigned 364-378 Died 378

  He was the younger brother of Valentinian I, who in 364 elevated him to the rank of co-emperor of the Roman Empire, granting him the rule of the Eastern provinces, while Valentinian retained the rule of the West. Both Valens and his brother were staunchly pro-Christian. After defeating the usurper Procopius in 366, Valens was at war with the Goths who sued for peace in 367 and pressed by the Huns asked for permission to cross the Danube into Roman territory. Regretting having granted this request to the untrustworthy and marauding Goths, Valens advanced against them in 378. His army was totally defeated and he died in the field.

"PROCOPIUS"
(*Procopius*)

Born 334   Reigned 365-366   Died 366

He accompanied Julian II as a commander of the army in the Persian campaign. He was entrusted by Jovian to conduct the dead body of Julian to Tarsus for interment. He led a rebellion against the unpopular Valens and was proclaimed emperor in Constantinople in 365. After a reign of only 8 months he was defeated by the forces of Valens and put to death.

"GRATIAN"
(*Flavius Gratianus*)

Born 359   Reigned 375-383   Died 383

He was the son of Valentinian I, and when only 8 years old was awarded the title of Augustus by his father. Upon his father's death in 375, Gratian became the emperor of the Western provinces after acknowledging as his colleague his half-brother Valentinian II, proclaimed Augustus by the legions, even though Gratian was only a young child. After the catastrophic defeat of Valens in 378, Gratian became emperor in the East. Hard pressed by the Goths he found it necessary to quickly call upon the services of his general Theodosius I whom he elevated as colleague in the East in 379. In 383 the usurper Magnus Maximus was proclaimed emperor by the legions in Britain and Gaul. Gratian setting out to confront Maximus was abandoned by his troops near Paris, fled south to Lyons where he was captured and killed. Maximus continued as master of Gaul, Spain, and Britain, until 388 when the soldier's of Theodosius I put him to death.

"VALENTINIAN II"
(*Flavius Valentinianus*)
Born 371   Reigned 375-392   Died 392

He was the son of Valentinian I, and the younger half-brother of Gratian with whom he was associated in governing the Western Empire upon the death of their father in 375, while Valens remained emperor in the East. Valentinian's rule included Italy, Illyricum, and Africa. Being a young child he was under the guardianship of the empress Justina, the second wife of Valentinian I. Gratian being about 10 years older was in fact the senior colleague in the West beyond the reach of his rule in Gaul, Spain, and Britain. After the death of Gratian, Magnus Maximus drove Valentinian II out of Italy but he was restored, this time as the sole emperor of the West by Theodosius after this Eastern ruling colleague defeated Maximus in 388. However, Valentinian miscalculating the loyalty of Arbogastes, his commander of the legions in Gaul, was repaid for his trust by being strangled on Arbogastes' order in 392.

" THEODOSIUS I, the GREAT "
(*Flavius Theodosius*)

Born ca. 346　　　　　Reigned 379-395　　　　　Died 395

   Theodosius was born in Spain the son of an able general Count Theodosius. Under Gratian he fought successfully against the Goths. Upon the death of Valens he was chosen to be the Gratian's colleague as Augustus in 379, and was awarded the rule of the Eastern Empire. He compelled the Goths to sue for peace and established a reproachment with the Persians. The murder of Gratian and the deposing of Valentinian II by Magnus Maximus required Theodosius to march against this usurper, and in 388 he finally defeated him and had him put to death, thus restoring the West to Valentinian. After putting down an insurrection in Thessalonica he allowed his troops to ravage the city and slay thousands of its inhabitants, an act that had him excommunicated by order of St. Ambrose and only after offering sincere penance was he readmitted to the fold. In 394 he subdued another usurper, Eugenius, a nominee of the traitorous Arbogastes, a general of Valentinian who had this prince put to death. In 383 Theodosius elevated his two sons Arcadius and Honorius to the rank of Augusti, with the intention that they rule as co-emperors over an Eastern and Western divided Empire. Theodosius died of dropsy in 395.

"FLACCILLA"
(*Aelia Flaccilla*)

Born ? Died 386

Flaccilla was the daughter of the prefect of Gaul, married Theodosius the Great as his first wife prior to his accession to the imperial throne. She was the mother of Arcadius and Honorius. Flaccilla was noted for her piety and generosity to the poor.

"EUGENIUS"
(*Eugenius*)
Born ?   Reigned 392-394   Died 394

Eugenius was of obscure birth but rose to be the palace guard of Valentinian II. He was proclaimed Augustus in Vienne in 392 following the murder of Valentinian by Arbogastes who retained virtual rule over the West and from this position of power engineered this elevation to the purple for Eugenius, intent on installing him essentially as a puppet emperor. Theodosius marched against the pair and in 394 won a decisive victory, captured Eugenius and had him put to death. The traitorous Arbogastes killed himself soon thereafter.

"ARCADIUS"
(*Flavius Arcadius*)

Born 377 Reigned 383 - 408 Died 408

He was the elder son of Theodosius I, who elevated him to the rank of Augustus in 383. On the death of Theodosius the Empire was divided between the two brothers, Arcadius receiving the Eastern provinces and Honorius the Western. Of weak character, Arcadius allowed the government to be directed by others. Died at Constantinople at the age of 31.

"HONORIUS"
(*Flavius Honorius*)

Born 384   Reigned 393 - 423   Died 423

The younger son of Theodosius I, elevated by his father to rank of Augustus at age 10. On the death of Theodosius he presided over the Western Empire, while his brother Arcadius governed the Eastern. Under this weak emperor, there was great turmoil, with numerous barbarian armies devastating all of the Western provinces, even to sacking Rome. These essentially unchecked advances by the marauding barbarian armies presaged the coming collapse of Roman rule in the Western Empire. Honorius died in Ravenna, after an inglorius reign, at age 39.

" GALLA PLACIDIA "
(*Galla Placidia*)

Born 388   Died 450

Galla Placidia was the daughter of Theodosius I, and half-sister of Arcadius and Honorius. After a troubled existence while held hostage after the taking of Rome by Alaric, she eventually was restored to Honorius and married Constantius III in 417. After the death of Constantius, she devoted her life to erecting and adorning sacred Christian buildings at Ravenna.

INDEX

Name	Page
AELIUS	51
AEMILIAN	105
AGRIPPA	17
AGRIPPINA, junior	26
AGRIPPINA, senior	23
AHENOBARBUS	4
ALLECTUS	132
ANTONINUS PIUS	52
ANTINOUS	50
ANTONIA	21
AQUILIA SEVERA	80
ARCADIUS	166
AUGUSTUS (OCTAVIAN)	13-15
AURELIAN	120
BALBINUS	91
BRITANNICUS	27
BRUTUS	3
CALIGULA	24
CARACALLA	73
CARAUSIUS	131
CARINUS	127
CARUS	125
CLAUDIUS	25
CLAUDIS II, GOTHICUS	118
CLEOPATRA	7, 8
CLODIUS ALBINUS	69
COMMODUS	60-62
CONSTANS	148
CONSTANTINE, the GREAT	143
CONSTANTINE II	147
CONSTANTIUS I, CHLORUS	135
CONSTANTIUS II	149
CONSTANTIUS GALLUS	155
CRISPINA	63
CRISPUS	146
DECENTIUS	152
DIADUMENIAN	77
DIDIA CLARA	67
DIDIUS JULIANUS	65
DIOCLETIAN	130
DOMITIA	38
DOMITIAN	37
DOMITILLA	34
DOMITIUS DOMITIANUS	133
DRUSUS, junior	19
DRUSUS, senior	20
ELAGABALUS	78
EUGENIUS	165
FAUSTA	145
FAUSTINA, junior	57
FAUSTINA, senior	53
FLACCILLA	165
FLORIANUS	123
GALBA	30
GALERIA VALERIA	137
GALERIUS	136
GALLA PLACIDIA	168
GALLIENUS	109
GERMANICUS	22
GETA	75
GORDIAN I, AFRICANUS	89
GORDIAN II, AFRICANUS	90
GORDIAN III	93
GRATIAN	161
HANNIBALLIANUS	150
HADRIAN	45-48
HELENA	144
HERENNIA ETRUSCILLA	101
HONORIUS	167
HOSTILIAN	102
JOTAPIAN	99
JOVIAN	157
JULIA DOMNA	71, 72
JULIA MAESA	82
JULIA MAMAEA	85
JULIA PAULA	79
JULIA SOAEMIAS	81
JULIA TITI	36
JULIAN, of PANNONIA	129
JULIAN II, the APOSTATE	156
JULIUS CAESAR	2
LABIENUS	5
LAELIANUS	114
LEPIDUS	10
LICINIUS I	142
LIVIA	16
LUCILLA	59
LUCIUS ANTONIUS	12
LUCIUS VERUS	58
MACRIANUS	112
MACRINUS	76
MAGNENTIUS	151
MAGNIA URBICA	128
MANLIA SCANTILLA	66
MARCIANA	42
MARCUS AURELIUS	54-56
MARINIANA	108
MARIUS	115
MARK ANTONY	9
MATIDIA	43

	PAGE		PAGE
MAXENTIUS	140	SABINA	49
MAXIMIANUS I, HERCULES	134	SALONINA	110
MAXIMINUS I, THRAX	86	SALONINUS	111
MAXIMINUS, DAZA	139	SEPTIMIUS SEVERUS	70
MAXIMUS	88	SEVERINA	121
NEPOTIAN	153	SEVERUS ALEXANDER	83
NERO	28, 29	SEVERUS II	138
NERVA	39	SEXTUS POMPEY	6
NUMERIAN	126	TACITUS	122
OCTAVIA	11	TETRICUS I	117
ORBIANA	84	THEODOSIUS I, the GREAT	160
OTACILIA SEVERA	96	TIBERIUS	18
OTHO	31	TITUS	35
PACATIAN	98	TRAJAN	40
PAULINA	87	TRAJAN DECIUS	100
PERTINAX	64	TRAJAN, PATER	44
PESCENNIUS NIGER	68	TRANQUILLINA	94
PHILIP I, the ARAB	95	TREBONIANUS GALLUS	103
PHILIP II	97	URANIUS ANTONINUS	106
PLAUTILLA	74	VALENS	159
PLOTINA	41	VALENTINIAN I	158
POMPEY, the GREAT	1	VALENTINIAN II	162
POSTUMUS	113	VALERIAN I	107
PROBUS	124	VESPASIAN	33
PROCOPIUS	160	VETRANIO	154
PUPIENUS	92	VICTORINUS	116
QUINTILLUS	119	VITELLIUS	32
ROMULUS	141	VOLUSIAN	104